"The ever-changing contours of race, religion, gender, and orientation are complex and difficult to traverse. In this work, Dr. Patrick Grant offers us a dynamic and thoughtful throughway that is scaffolded by scholarship and guided with love. It is a necessary exploration of these intersecting worlds that is important to our collective journey towards sexual equity and liberation."

–**Shadeen Francis,** LMFT, CST; The People's Therapy Group

"Grant has beautifully constructed an essential guide that allows all of us to challenge the limiting beliefs we have internalized around Black same gender loving men. This text is for anyone seeking personal and professional growth and healing from oppressive homonegative myths that separate us from each other and ourselves."

–**Dalychia Saah,** Afrosexology.com; Brown School of Social Work, Washington University in St. Louis

"Dr. Grant has given us a thoughtful exploration of sexual diversity in the Black communities, especially the impact of negativity on people's health and well-being. Using phenomenological interviews, Dr. Grant amplifies the voices of Black same-gender loving men, combining his research and clinical work with his life experience to create a deep reflection of culture, race, and sexuality."

–**Richard A. Sprott,** PhD; President of the Society for the Psychology of Sexual Orientation and Gender Diversity, 2021–2022, APA Division 44, Department of Human Development and Women's Studies, California State University, East Bay

Internalized Homonegativity Among Same Gender Loving Black Men

This book accessibly explores the phenomenon of internalized homonegativity among same gender loving Black men who love other men, providing practical tools to help therapists identify the underlying motivations for their clients' feelings.

Written from personal and clinical experience, P. Ryan Grant defines internalized homonegativity as the negative thoughts felt by a person due to their same gender loving identity. The book's introduction provides a backdrop of the developmental experiences Black same gender loving men often encounter and connects theoretical concepts with qualitative Black same gender loving male experiences. Chapters then explore the contextual consequences of internalized homonegativity and educate readers on how conditioned shame and anxiety relating to these factors alter mental health and functioning in various spaces. The final part of the book presents therapeutic techniques based on dialectical behavior therapy (DBT), cognitive-behavioral therapy (CBT), and acceptance and commitment therapy (ACT) to assist readers in helping clients navigate a homonegative world.

This book is essential reading for sex therapists, educators, students, and sexuality professionals who are looking for resources on working with Black same gender loving male clients, as well as those in occupations seeking to create programs for Black same gender loving men. It will also be a helpful resource for Black same gender loving men seeking to live value-based lives.

P. Ryan Grant, MPH, PsyD, is a clinical psychology postdoctoral resident whose interests include examining, affirming, and improving sexual and mental wellness within the Black community.

Leading Conversations on Black Sexualities and Identities

Series editors: James C. Wadley

Leading Conversations in Black Sexualities and Identities aims to stimulate sensitive conversations and teachings surrounding Black sexuality. Written by academics and practitioners who have dedicated their work to the distinctive sexual and relational experiences of persons of African descent, the series aims to provoke an enhanced understanding throughout the field of sexology and identify educational and clinical strategies for change. Amplifying issues and voices often minimalized and marginalized, this series is a continuation and expansion of inquiry and advocacy upon the complexities and nuances of relational negotiation, identity affirmation, critical discourse, and liberated sexual expression.

Titles in the series:

Internalized Homonegativity Among Same Gender Loving Black Men: An Exploration of Truths
P. Ryan Grant

Sexual Health and Black College Students: Exploring the Sexual Milieu of HBCUs
Naomi M. Hall

Black Women, Intersectionality, and Workplace Bullying: Intersecting Distress
Leah P. Hollis

Internalized Homonegativity Among Same Gender Loving Black Men

An Exploration of Truths

P. Ryan Grant

R Routledge
Taylor & Francis Group

NEW YORK AND LONDON

First published 2023
by Routledge
605 Third Avenue, New York, NY 10158

and by Routledge
4 Park Square, Milton Park, Abingdon, Oxon, OX14 4RN

*Routledge is an imprint of the Taylor & Francis Group, an
informa business*

Library of Congress Cataloging-in-Publication Data
A catalog record for this title has been requested

ISBN: 978-1-032-01573-6 (hbk)
ISBN: 978-1-032-20686-8 (pbk)
ISBN: 978-1-003-18093-7 (ebk)

DOI: 10.4324/9781003180937

Typeset in Times New Roman
by MPS Limited, Dehradun

Contents

Acknowledgments

Giving glory and honor to the Creator for using me, a sensitive and shy child of immigrants, to increase awareness of Black same gender loving male experiences.

I acknowledge the Jamaican national hero, Nanny of the Maroons, whose story reminds me of the power in resisting and dismantling systems of white supremacy.

I thank my family—Patrick Grant, Zetta Grant, and Patrice Grant—for their love and support, which has strengthened my voice and pushed me towards a life of advocacy and honesty.

I thank Dr. James Wadley, PhD, for his mentorship, which has pushed me to reach higher and seek greater. I don't know where my work would be without his encouragement and guidance. I thank Dr. Michael Sude, PhD, and Dr. Julie Hill, PhD, whose support and collaboration led to the completion and expansion of my dissertation.

I thank my peers, dear friends, and sisters in sexuality, Dalychia Saah, MSW, Rafaella Smith-Fiallo, MSW, LCSW, and Shadeen Francis, LMFT, CST. Your presence rejuvenates and your work inspires. Thank you for being my co-conspirators in the efforts toward Black sexual liberation.

To the men of Alpha Phi Alpha Fraternity, Inc.—specifically Bro. Rev. Darrell Tiller, Bro. Dr. James E. Davis, Bro. Sterling Grimes, Bro. Eric Cole, Bro. Albert C. Bristol, Bro. Otha E. Thornton, and Bro. Jonas Crenshaw. Thank you for teaching me about brotherhood, continuously pushing me to excavate my truths, and encouraging me to take up space.

To Bryce L. Carmichael, Chelsea P. Freeman, Erica Philpot, Megan E. Lawrence, Michelle Gordon, Rahel Boghossian, and Tanya Dastyar. Thank you for giving me the gift of true friendship.

Finally, eternal gratitude to the courageous Black same gender loving men who have brought (and continue to bring) nuance to this work by sharing their lived experiences. I honor you and dedicate my life's work to you.

Foreword

When I first met Dr. Patrick Grant several years ago, he had just started his doctoral journey at LaSalle University in Philadelphia. Creative, imaginative, eloquent, and intellectually curious, he shared with me some of his struggles in the field as a young African American same gender loving male student and researcher. We talked about the invisibility and lack of mentorship of young Black men and how pervasive homonegative attitudes impact the social, emotional, and professional development of this population. What I appreciated most about Patrick was his willingness to share his experiences with me and talk through some of the challenges that he had faced as a young professional.

Over the years, Patrick has grown immensely into an insightful and strategic scholar who has given visibility and voice to same gender loving (SGL) Black men through his leadership, research, social media activity, and clinical intuition. I am blessed and privileged to be a part of this first Black sexuality exegesis offered by Dr. Grant as he offers us a compelling narrative, *Internalized Homonegativity among Black Same Gender Loving Men: An Exploration of Truths.* What is profound about this work, is that Patrick was able to capture some of the life experiences of Black same gender loving men in a manner that showcases their vulnerability and truths. He tells a portion of their story by intertwining his story in a manner that is graceful, provocative, candid, and revealing. Moreover, when he shared with me his thoughts about minority stress theory (Meyer, 2003) and critical race theory (Delgado, Sefancic, & Harris, 2017), and how they may impact the life experiences of Black "bottoms," I was intrigued because I knew that there was relatively no literature that had addressed the confluence of race, gender, power, identity, and sexuality for this population. In my eight years of serving as Editor-in-Chief for the *Journal of Black Sexuality and Relationships* and founder of the Association of Black Sexologists and Clinicians, I am certain that this work moves the field in a manner that pushes us to move past our own homonegativity to support and celebrate the relational and sexual experiences of Black same gender loving men. *As a field, we needed someone like Dr. Patrick Grant to lead the conversation about the continuum of Black sexualities and identities as it relates to the experiences of the same loving men* and I am ecstatic that he has chosen to share this moment and this movement with us.

Dr. Grant gives us a gift with this work and I am immensely proud of him for creating the space for all of us to learn and grow from his scholarship.

James C. Wadley, PhD, Series Editor

References

Delgado, R., Stefancic, J., & Harris, A. P. (2017). *Critical race theory: An introduction* (3rd ed.). New York: New York University Press.

Meyer, I. H. (2003). Prejudice, social stress, and mental health in lesbian, gay, and bisexual populations: Conceptual issues and research evidence. *Psychological Bulletin, 129*(5), 674–697. 10.1037/0033-2909.129.5.674

Introduction

Five months before writing this text, I was a 29-year-old, same gender loving, Black man, on his way to acquiring a doctorate in clinical psychology, who exemplified how one could thrive after rejecting homonegativity and finding security in their sexual identity. I overcame the obstacles one may face as a Black person traversing academia; I also conquered the sexual- and gender-based obstacles one may face as a same gender loving individual existing in various spaces within the Black community—the Black church, Black fraternal space, and the Black family. I had arrived! I thought myself to have reached a zenith of enlightenment. I bought into the idea that I had reached some height of Black same-gender lovingness—a pinnacle of sexual identity that now afforded me the skillset to guide others to freedom, liberation, and self-acceptance. I elevated myself on media platforms and used my writings and research to provide same gender loving men, struggling with their sexual identities, an example of the sexual, interpersonal, spiritual, and other changes that could occur when one embraces and affirms their sexual and romantic identities. I openly shared my explorations of gender expression in order to communicate that masculinity—specifically, Black masculinity—can be nuanced, varied, and complex. Yet despite these efforts, I possessed a blind spot.

Before being debuted to the world as an identity-affirming psychologist, I elected to participate in mental health therapy. I initially sought out therapy to improve my skill as a clinician—to "experience therapy from the other side." I saw myself as one who, despite existing in environments that used homonegativity to oppress my mind, body, and spirit, was able to overcome and achieve more than I could imagine. I utilized my accomplishments to assert myself as a Black same gender loving liberator who had successfully obtained personal freedom and was now equipped to unshackle other Black same gender loving men through research and clinical practice. I was so convinced

DOI: 10.4324/9781003180937-1

that "I had made it" as a Black same gender loving man that, in one of my therapy sessions, I inquired whether I truly ever internalized the homonegativity I experienced from my environments. I was blind to my own truth.

My truth is that I have achieved academic and professional successes throughout these now 30 years of life. I have used intellect and research, degrees, and academic decorations as tools to position myself as an expert in Black sexuality and gender. I have learned to interpersonally engage in diverse spheres, which has afforded me the opportunity, access, and privilege to show up as authentically and inauthentically as I desire. My truth includes that I have engaged myself in various forms of internal and external rebranding, however genuine, in order to advance in a world that devalues me based on my covert and overt identities. The accomplishments I have made in this lifetime serve as tools that have helped me survive in spaces that have judged and berated me just for existing. My liberative stances on sexuality and gender stem from years of resisting environments that have attempted to "kick me back in the closet" prior to my awareness of the closet and its functions.

The successes amassed in my 30 years shield a young Black boy who was labeled "gay" by church members before he possessed any understanding of sex and sexuality. The free and confident expressions I exude are traits I quickly adopted in order to escape the physical, mental, emotional, and spiritual danger I experienced throughout my primary and secondary education by peers—trauma experiences I neatly tucked away and only uncovered with multiple individual therapy sessions. There are aspects of my being that are healed and that remain soft, powerful, and thriving. There are also parts of me that are hurt, hardened, and learning to live beyond survival mode. While I use the access that comes from academic accomplishment to aid in uplifting my communities, I occasionally navigate in ways that perpetuate the oppressive scripts I seek to dismantle. I am always moving forward in the holistic liberation of Black same gender loving men, yet my thoughts, emotions, and actions are continuously informed and impacted by past experiences that have sought to extinguish my same gender loving Black gay male light. My truth is that I hold—now and for the rest of my days—many intersecting truths that have, that do, and that will inform the ways I show up in various spaces.

In 2016, the critically acclaimed film, *Moonlight* (storied by Tarrell Alvin McCraney and directed by Barry Jenkins), captured the attention and praise of vast audiences (Jenkins, 2016; Scott, 2016). Many applauded the film for seemingly providing the first mainstream representation of Black same gender loving male development through its main character Chiron (played by Alex Hibbert, Ashton Sanders, and Trevante Rhodes). Others lauded the film for depicting various facets of the Black experience that have been sustained in the United States by structural and institutional capitalist and White supremacist efforts (Scott, 2016). While these perspectives emphasize the interpretable nature of the film, I introduce *Moonlight* in a work that explores internalized homonegativity among Black same gender loving men to highlight the themes woven within the main character's development and introduce the exploration of Black male sexual identity development.

Viewers of *Moonlight* are first introduced to Chiron as a young boy who desperately tries to escape the violent pursuit of peers in his neighborhood. This desire to escape leads Chiron to hide in an abandoned "dope house" until his assailants have disappeared. The imagery of Chiron covering his ears while surrounded by indecipherable noise draws pathos-laden parallels to experiences had by many same gender loving Black men throughout their lives—experiences that involve feeling ostracized and confused by the perceptions, opinions, and enacted violences of those who identify a socially constructed deficit in these men in order to justify their harm. The movie continues this parallel as the young Chiron (nicknamed "Little"), who is often silent throughout the film, uses his voice in moments of safety to ask, "What is a faggot?" "Am I a faggot?" and "How do I know?" Chiron's questioning mirrors the thoughts many Black same gender loving men have explored in efforts to understand their existence and experiences.

As he tries to understand his identities throughout the film—which includes processing both his sexuality and conceptualizations of manhood—Chiron interacts with the characters Juan and Kevin, who serve as two guides throughout his journey. Juan, the first principal character to be introduced in the film, presents as the epitome of what some may deem balanced masculinity (Hui & Jackson, 2017; McGuire, Berhanu, Davis, & Harper, 2014; Pelzer, 2016). He is well respected in his community, holds power through his profession, serves as a literal and metaphoric protector and provider, and allows himself room to experience an emotional vulnerability that appears when he is confronted with the ways his drug distribution impacts his community and those he loves. One of the most powerful scenes in the film appears when Juan, who becomes a father figure to Chiron, takes Chiron to the beach and teaches him how to swim. While this scene highlights a Black father–son interaction that serves as a corrective experience in young Chiron's journey, there are spiritual themes that arise which speak to Chiron's development throughout the film. Juan facilitates a metaphoric baptism, in which Chiron washes away the sins of help-lessness and confusion that have come from the sexual and gender identity-based degradation he has experienced from his environment. Chiron consequently emerges a new creature as Juan encourages him, to "decide who [he] is going to be."

Despite the freedom Chiron is given by Juan, Chiron's relationship with Kevin (played by Jaden Piner, Jharrell Jerome, and Andre Holland) quickly reveals that Chiron remains trapped in navigating gender and sexuality with his environment. Juxtaposing the openness he experiences with Juan, Chiron volleys between moments of vulnerability and masculine performance with Kevin, as Kevin teaches Chiron that he must "show people he is not soft." Yet it is also with Kevin that Chiron openly expresses that he "cries so much… [he] feels [he will] turn into drops." Despite this intimacy, Kevin's adherence to masculine scripts eventually leads him to betray Chiron through a public display of physical violence. The pain from Kevin's betrayal transforms Chiron into a stereotyped presentation of Black masculinity—a presentation that equates Black manhood with physical prowess, emotional repres-sion, and an exoticism that elicits both attraction and fear from the white gaze. Chiron, after his betrayal, immerses himself in the white-constructed truth of Black masculinity in order to survive the com-pounded traumas he has endured from his environment.

Throughout the film, Chiron poses many questions yet provides no concrete answers to these inquiries, which allows viewers the chance to make assumptions about his developed truths. Viewers cannot con-cretely state whether Chiron identifies as gay, bisexual, queer, or same gender loving. It is also unclear whether Chron's gender presentation in adulthood is congruent with his inner identity. Viewers are also unaware of whether Chiron explicitly experiences internalized homo-negativity, although throughout the film he exudes traits that depict isolation and emotional distress resultant from others' response to his perceived incongruence with masculinity.

Although Chiron's upbringing contrasts with my own, there are si-milarities between our experiences that parallel a process of sexual identity development endured by other Black same gender loving men. The external environments that nurtured Chiron and I were steeped in homonegativity; and like Chiron, I learned I could construct certain truths and presentations to survive these homonegative spaces.

Also congruent with Chiron's experience is the ambivalence and discomfort I held toward my same-gender attractions, which directly stemmed from the homonegative environments that nurtured me. Such reflects the experiences of many Black same gender loving men—existing in homonegative environments that foster the propagation of internalized homonegativity; adopting tools throughout the lifespan that aid in the service of survival; contriving portrayals of masculine performance that prove to a homophobic world that one's sexual identity does not deter their overall functioning. Yet these survival tactics do not lead to affirmed identity. They only reinforce and justify the cycle of subordinating same gender loving identity.

Conceptualization of homonegativity and its uses

It is my hope that individuals from diverse backgrounds will take interest in how homonegativity impacts sexual identities and expressions, as well as in the specific ways Black same gender loving men experience, and are impacted by, internalized homonegativity. As this work is being primarily disseminated through academia, I hope that professionals—therapeutic counselors and clinicians, medical professionals, social justice advocates, sex workers, and those who work within and influence law, politics, and policies—can use this analysis to understand the systemic precipitants and multifaceted consequences of internalized homonegativity, and use this understanding to transform their spheres of influence and make their domains safe for Black same gender loving men to identify, explore, express, and demonstrate understanding of their own relationships with internalized homonegativity. I hope to disrupt the dynamic in which privileged individuals—for the purpose of this book, anyone who is not a Black same gender loving man—survey Black same gender loving male experiences in a voyeuristic manner, which leads to the increased marginalization of this group via the continuation of oppressive traditions (e.g., Black same gender loving men being positioned as props, objects of micro-aggressive observation, mules for intellectual labor, or case studies of Black resilience) (Ross, 2013). This work intends to help all readers confront their relationships with white supremacist ideals (i.e., homonegativity and its related phenomena) and investigate the ways in which these relationships influence their interactions with, and intentions toward, Black same gender loving men.

The current exploration of Black same gender loving male internalized homonegativity will not overly focus on coming out. Coming out (i.e., the process by which one publicly announces and displays their sexual and romantic attractions in various public arenas) has been conceptualized by mainstream culture as somewhat of a zenith of sexual development in which gay folx are shown "to be simply 'men and women whose homosexuality is irrelevant to [their] ideals, principles, hopes and aspirations" (Faderman, 2016). It is not uncommon to witness the promotion of coming out as a marker of individual and communal/social progress. National Coming Out Day, evidence of this promotion, is an annual occurrence that was started by Robert Eichsberg and Jean O'Leary in 1988 to commemorate the Second National March on Washington for Gay Rights, which occurred on October 11, 1987 (Faderman, 2016; George Mason University). Currently, individuals and organizations use October 11th (or a surrounding date) to highlight the undeniable presence of gay people in society. While well-meaning and assumingly affirming of lesbian, gay, bisexual, and other (LGB+) communities, the current gay liberation movement (which was ignited in 1969 by two trans women of color, Marsha P. Johnson and Sylvia Rivera) is often blind to the systemic and social needs of Black people (i.e., financial and social equity, social safety, adequate and validating healthcare), including same gender loving Black men (Nelson, Pantalone, & Carey, 2019; Nero, 2005). Further, research suggests that the Black community's historically conditioned approach to sexuality (to be explored in subsequent parts of this book) makes coming out a low prioritized, and somewhat risky, behavior for many Black men. I therefore do not present coming out as an idealized goal or purpose that drives this work (McCune, 2014). My research, which qualitatively explores same gender loving Black male experiences with internalized homonegativity, also suggests that "one does not overcome internalized homonegativity by coming out" (Grant, 2020b). This work will transcend coming out and focus on expanding same gender loving Black male truths.

I am afforded the opportunity to explore an experience that appears in the lives of all same gender loving Black men to some degree. I therefore intended to use my privilege, access, and knowledge to provide increased knowledge, access, awareness, and resource to Black same gender loving men who struggle with holding and understanding their relationships with external and internalized homonegativity. Academic, scientific, and other spheres have historically amassed quantitative, qualitative, and mixed methods data on same gender loving Black men that frequently circulate in ivory-towered spaces (i.e., escapist spaces, often educational, in which community problems are discussed, yet practical solutions and resources are rarely uncovered). This data often does not reach the populations it is intended to serve and is frequently expected to have a trickle-down impact through funding and well-intentioned, yet unsustainable, community programming (Hoefer & Hoefer, 2017; Nelson, Pantalone, & Carey, 2019). The historic disparities in housing, finance, healthcare, and education between Black same gender loving men and their white counterparts highlight the juxtaposition between the oversaturated examination of, and underapplied practical care given to, Black same gender loving men (Lewis, 2003; Mays, Cochran, & Barnes, 2007; Nelson, Pantalone, & Carey, 2019; Nero, 2005; Stone & Ward, 2011; Ward, 2008). In order to interrupt this pattern, the current text critically analyzes internalized homonegativity to identify achievable practices that influence the increased exposure to, and understanding of, internalized homonegativity among Black same gender loving men.

Although mainstream culture often positions Black same gender loving men as monolithic, Black same gender loving men are multifaceted beings who vary in size, shape, sensibility, demeanor, and purpose; beings whose lived experiences encompass limitless truths. The current text uses extant literature, current events, media, and qualitative interviews to explicitly highlight some of these truths. Readers will be engaged with questions and behavioral practices to assist them in confronting their truths related to sexual identity, internalized homonegativity, and Black same gender loving male experiences. It is possible that some readers' truths may not be found in this work but may be developed by processing the information provided in this text. Whatever the experience one has with the book, it is my hope that Black same gender loving men fundamentally use this resource as a tool to gain a greater understanding of their sexual and romantic identities, their lived experiences, and relationships with internalized homonegativity.

Why Black same gender loving men?

Although social progressions have arisen to benefit same-sex attracted individuals, some same gender loving Black men still struggle to affirm their identities in numerous spaces (McCune, 2008, 2014; Snorton, 2014). Risk and negative consequences still exist for some Black same gender loving men who choose to internally accept, and externally express, their same gender loving identities (Beam, 2008; Johnson, 2014). Some of these consequences include, yet are not limited to, familial rejection, religious and social ostracization, and privilege restriction (Beam, 2008; Boykin, & Shange, 2012; Johnson, 2014; Tennial, 2015). These consequences, however, do not reflect the innate values of the Black community; they are instead reinforced outcomes that have roots in white supremacy and the conditioning of Black thoughts and values within a white supremacist framework (Boykin, 2006; hooks, 2004; Poulson-Bryant, 2006). This text can be used as a tool to help folx—professional and lay—understand the oppressive frameworks that contribute to the experience of internalized homonegativity among Black same gender loving men. It is my intention that this work will also provide techniques, frameworks, and guided questions that will assist Black same gender loving men in transcending oppressive structures and pursuing value-based living.

The term "same gender loving" (SGL) is used throughout this text to describe cisgender Black men who have sexual or romantic attractions to other cisgender Black men. As an act of resistance during a Million Black Men March in the 1990s—an event that touts concern for the Black community while promoting homonegative practices and beliefs—Cleo Manago introduced "same gender loving" to describe Black people who are sexually and romantically attracted to those of the same gender. For many Black same gender loving men, labels such as gay, bisexual, and queer are associated with trauma and have often been accompanied by social ostracization, disenfranchisement, and physical, mental, and emotional violence (Manago, 1996). My work with Black men and their experiences of homonegativity exposed a trend in which many of the men proudly owned their sexual and romantic desires for other men, yet effortfully resisted being associated with labels such as gay, bisexual, queer, and MSM (the label "men who have sex with men [MSM]" is oftentimes used in scientific spaces that research Black male navigations of HIV). In using same gender loving/SGL, I hope to facilitate a safety in this book that will allow readers to see themselves, pair their narratives and histories with the narratives and histories presented, and use the resources provided in this work to live lives that honor their identities.

A foundational tenet of this work includes the tapestrying of Black same gender loving male narratives throughout the text to support the suggestions presented about homonegativity and Black SGL life. To be a Black same gender loving person—a Black same gender loving man—is to be connected to the historical, ancestral, and communal resistance that has carried Black folx throughout centuries, and to share in an experience of knowing joy and love despite ever-present experiences of pain and fear; it is to be a member of a people who have found freedom and safety amid experiences of hypervigilance to violence and danger. My research findings on Black same gender loving male experiences provide evidence of why members of this resilient cohort may seek and benefit from the present work (Grant, 2016, 2018, 2020a, 2020b). Many Black same gender loving men have overcome obstacles related to their sexual and romantic attractions, and have developed the fortitude to survive, yet still need tools to navigate a homonegative world. Some Black SGL men have noticed the challenges endured by other Black same gender loving men and may seek to be better equipped in their advocacy and communal support (Grant, 2020b); and others hold general curiosities regarding the ways Black same gender loving men have become associated with homonegativity-laden phenomena such as down low (DL) culture, trauma narratives, poor mental health outcomes, risky sexual and other behavior, and the acquisition and proliferation of the human immunodeficiency virus (HIV) (Boykin, 2006; Grant, 2018, 2020b; Griffin, 2010; Johnson, 2014; McCune, 2014; Snorton, 2014). Whatever the experience, perspective, and conceptualizations that have brought readers to this text, this work will promote the engaging of literature, reflection, and lived experience to assist Black same gender loving male readers in reclaiming their power, holding their fullness, and creating lives that honor their truths.

In conducting this work, I have reflected on what offerings would be most relevant and accessible to those who work with, and for, Black same gender loving men, as well as those who may not work with Black same gender loving men yet have an interest in the present topic. I therefore include four elements throughout this book that broaden its reach and applicability:

- Narrative: Qualitative narrative is a powerful tool that can increase understanding of phenomena, particularly when the said phenomena is understudied. I volley between providing my personal narrative, and the narratives of Black same gender loving men I interviewed through a hermeneutic phenomenological qualitative research design, to collect and present data on internalized homonegativity among Black same gender loving men (Barker, Pistrang, & Elliot, 2016; Kafle, 2013; Mack et al., 2005; VanManen, 1990). This method brings a unique and personal voice that honors the experiences depicted throughout the text and centers Black same gender loving men, rather than extant research or literature, as the focus of this work.
- Literature: As past research has used Black same gender loving male experiences to support and bring relevance to its findings, this work uses relevant research and literature (labeled "truths") to support and complement the presented qualitative experiences of Black same gender loving men.
- Reflection: Through my work, I developed and used an open-ended

protocol to collect qualitative data on Black same gender loving male experiences. This protocol has triggered deep reflection in my participants and has helped them to uncover various aspects of their relationship to homonegativity. In this text, I have provided process questions, under the heading "What is your truth?" in order to assist readers in confronting their own experiences with internalized and externalized homonegativity. Such reflection will be useful in helping clinicians, trainees, and advocates uncover blind spots in their work. These questions will also help Black same gender loving men and their loved ones further reflect on their relationships with, and consequential reactions to, homonegativity.

• Clinical Consideration: Scattered throughout this text are tips and considerations that can aid clinicians and those who work with Black same gender loving men in assessing, treating, and further understanding various aspects of internalized homonegativity.

By understanding the general outline of this work, readers are now prepared to delve into the experiences of Black same gender loving men.

On being a black same gender loving man...

It means being liberated in a world where people have been told they can't be same gender loving, particularly as a Black man; being told that is something one shouldn't be joyful of, or proud of, or inspired by. In this moment it's a site of liberation and freedom.

Simeon, 31, Brooklyn, NY

This is just a part of me. I'm a Black man before I'm gay, and I'm a man before I'm a Black man. For so long, I used to think that this was all that I was, but it's not all anyone is. I think why so many of us don't accept it is because we think, "This is all I am. Gay, gay, gay, I'm just gay!"

Avery, 33, Washington, D.C.

Fear is the one emotion I remember feeling the most. I wanted to pray and rebuke the gayness away because I wanted to be accepted and loved. I wanted my mom to look at me with fullness and not see me as someone who was incomplete. Of course, that didn't work and over time I had to come to love and embrace myself.

Marcus, 35, Clifton, MD

It's freedom, expression, comfort, and security.

Edgar, 30, Lawnside, NJ

To me currently, I think it's multilayered. There's a part of me that is super excited about being who I am as a Black man, same sex attracted; but there's also a level of discomfort, a level of uncertainty. There are a lot of things I think about and go back and forth on, that I'm nervous about. I would say a melting pot of questions and reflections.

MJ, 30, Charlotte, NC

What's your truth?

• In general, what are your positive and negative views of same gender loving folx?

• What are your views and assumptions (positive and negative) of cisgender Black men? How have these views impacted your engagement with this group?

1 Internalized Homonegativity: Back to Basics

Internalized homonegativity

Homonegativity is used throughout this work to describe negative attitudes—thoughts and appraisals, prejudices, discomforts, emotions, responses, and reactions—a person (a same gender loving Black man) may possess toward same gender lovingness. Internalized homonegativity captures a process in which the negative attitudes toward non-heterosexuality are directed inward when Black same gender loving men (the focus of this work) recognize their own same gender loving status. Internalized homonegativity also reflects a dynamic in which negative appraisals of same gender loving attraction are learned and absorbed from external environments (a process to be explored throughout this work). It is useful to distinguish internalized homonegativity from the commonly conflated concept of internalized homophobia. While many use these terms interchangeably, homophobia has often been used in discussions of sexual orientation to describe anxious, avoidant, responses to perceived homosexuality. This may appear through the bullying of same gender loving persons; the perpetuation of hate crimes toward those who are same gender loving; or the enaction of rules, laws, and institutions that do not support same gender loving advancement. However, many contemporaries argue that the term "homophobia" does not fully capture the oppression of the same gender loving folx as thoroughly as homonegativity.

Gregory Herek (2000, 2015) emphasizes that prejudice toward same gender loving people and practices does not necessarily denote phobia. He reminds us that a phobia involves a clear, occasionally debilitating, irrational fear targeted toward an object or situation (Herek 2000, 2015). Many individuals and systems have expressed prejudices toward same gender loving folx without being afraid of same gender loving people, practices, and presentations. Herek describes that those who

DOI: 10.4324/9781003180937-2

possess phobias often seek assistance in managing, reducing, or curing their phobic experience. This point is particularly important in moving away from the term "homophobia," as most "homophobes" have no interest in changing their damaging and oppressive ideologies (Herek, 2015).

Additionally, Herek (2015) notes that while phobias are centered around and fueled by the endorsing of irrational beliefs, many beliefs maintained by "homophobes" are not scientifically irrational. For example, while same gender loving folx are not dangerous, fears endorsed by people who hold homonegative views (e.g., the fear that proximity to same gender loving people or practices will prompt one to confront their thoughts about, or relationship to, same gender loving folx) are valid and cannot be conceptualized as irrationality (Herek, 2015).

Herek (2015) further presents homophobia's inability to fully capture the negative feelings toward same gender loving people and practices by highlighting how this term does not account for institutional oppression, independently held prejudices toward SGL folx, and self-hate internalized by same gender loving people. Herek (2015) invites us to consider stigma—the social negative appraisal of those who possess demographic differences—as we scrutinize homophobia and distinguish homonegativity from homophobia. He describes how those who possess demographic differences are either made invisible and relegated to social margins or positioned as objects of social hostility when their differences become increasingly visible to the majority gaze (Herek, 2015). Herek (2000) offers *sexual prejudice* to describe the negative attitudes targeted toward non-heterosexuals; and provides *structural sexual stigma* as the entity that enforces social, institutional, interpersonal, financial, and other power differentials between heterosexual and non-heterosexuals. It is in the space between structural sexual stigma and sexual prejudice that homonegativity exists. Negative attitudes toward same gender loving identities and behaviors are insidious frames of thought that privilege heteronormative presentations and marginalize anything which presents as non-heterosexual. Homonegativity is a phenomenon that exists in external (e.g., in families, social groups, religious spaces, law) and internal (e.g., in thoughts and emotions) environments and can be engaged and expressed by heterosexuals and non-heterosexuals.

Homonegativity is a more insidious form of homophobia that transcends the conceptualization of anxiety and avoidance. Homonegativity lays the foundation for the manifestation of homophobic violence. Homonegativity is begotten from common perceptions of "normality"—the idea that this world is naturally constructed through binaries that designate the typical and atypical, holy and sinful, intellectual and base, privileged and oppressed (Blank, 2012; Foucault, 2012; Collins, 2004). Homonegativity is a consequence of white supremacy that constructs social castes and rations privileges based on one's ability to adhere to presentations that align with white, Christian, heterosexual, able-bodied, educated, wealthy, cisgender, male ideals (Blank 2012; Collins, 2004). Homonegativity is a puritanical and elitist farce many Black folx have engaged and internalized as a result of centuries' old Western oppression that has placed Black people in constant bargaining for their humanity (Blank, 2012; Collins, 2004). To echo Patricia Hill Collins (2004), issues of Black sexuality cannot be addressed without acknowledging the impacts of racism. Black same gender loving male experiences with homonegativity cannot be explored without highlighting how Black marginalization based on race has created space for Black marginalization based on sexual orientation; and as the call is made for systems that oppress sexual minorities to be lifted, the call against racial oppression must also resound (Crenshaw, 1989; Delgado, Stefancic, & Harris, 2017; Collins, 2004; Collins & Bilge, 2020).

Despite the appropriateness of homonegativity to depict the negative appraisals of non-heterosexual individuals, behaviors, and practices, scholars have presented heterosexism as a term that addresses the individual, institutional, social, and cultural forms of the same gender loving stigmatization that demonize and belittle same gender loving people, practices, and presentations (Berg, Munthe-Kaas, & Ross, 2016; Meyer, 1995; Szymanski, Kashubeck-West, & Meyer, 2008; Trujillo, Perrin, Henry, & Rabinovitch, 2020). Recent literature often replaces homonegativity with heterosexism and has asserted that heterosexism captures the way same gender loving lives are systemically impacted by more than negative attitudes (Berg, Munthe-Kaas, & Ross, 2016; Meyer, 1995; Szymanski, Kashubeck-West, & Meyer, 2008; Trujillo, Perrin, Henry, & Rabinovitch, 2020). I, however, call for a shift in the zeitgeist, as cognitive-behavioral frameworks reinforce that institutional, social, and cultural norms arise from individual belief (Beck, 2011). Systemic oppression has no power without collectively endorsed individual beliefs. Further, while heterosexism may capture the breadth of white gay, lesbian, and bisexual experiences, homonegativity is apt when speaking about the internalized experiences of the same gender loving Black men, as it is my belief that one cannot fully embody an oppressive construct from which one cannot fully benefit. When conceptualizing race, some acknowledge that while Black folx can perpetuate racism and anti-Blackness, they cannot be racist as they will never benefit from the system of racism (Blay, 2015). Likewise, while same gender loving Black men can perpetuate heterosexism, their race and sexual and romantic identities prevent them from entirely embodying and benefitting from heterosexism; at best, same gender loving Black men may only contribute to heterosexist systems through homonegative thought and practice.

What's your truth?

• What are your thoughts about homonegativity?
• How have you engaged with, or experienced, homonegativity in your life?

Homonegativity, at its surface, centers on sexual orientation. Yet in order to understand homonegativity, one must grasp the complex relationships between biological sex, gender identity, gender expression, and sexual orientation. These qualities are not fixed, yet in adherence to prevailing conceptions of normalcy, society (through medicine, law, politics, education, etc.) has exerted an effort to present biological sex, gender identity and expression, and sexual orientation as fixed binaries (Creighton, 2001; Fausto-Sterling, 2020; Money, Hampson, & Hampson, 1955, 1957; Phornphutkul, Boney, Fausto-Sterling, & Gruppuso, 1998). These variables then serve as schemas (i.e., mental shortcuts) which enable the general population to use quick assumptions to classify individuals based on their presentations (Rosenthal, 2013; Yarber & Sayad, 2018). These schemas prove to be dangerous, as history highlights the ways erroneously simplified observations such as "Black and male," "Black, male, and urban," "Black, seemingly male, and wearing makeup," can lead to the development of biased heuristics (i.e., judgments made from the accessing of schemas) that make room for the oppression, marginalization, and the perpetuation of psychical, mental, psychological, emotional, or spiritual violence toward diverse groups (Barvosa, 2014; Mereish, Sheskier, Hawthorne, & Goldbach, 2019).

Biological sex

Biological sex attempts to label individuals as male or female based on their genetic and anatomical presentations. If one is born with XY chromosomes and a visible penis, or if testosterone dominates one's hormonal makeup, one would be assigned as having been born into the world as male (Rosenthal, 2013; Stoller, 1990; Yarber & Sayad, 2018).

If one is born with XX chromosomes and a visible vulva, or produces more estrogen than testosterone throughout the lifespan, one is likely to be classified as an individual born female (Rosenthal, 2013; Yarber & Sayad, 2018). However, science informs us that biological sex is much more fluid, as there exist those with variance in their genetic and anatomical expressions (Rosenthal, 2013; Yarber & Sayad, 2018). Those who are intersex cannot be quickly categorized, as they possess what medical communities have deemed to be "ambiguous genitalia" (Rosenthal, 2013). Those with Androgen Insensitivity Syndrome (AIS) possess XY chromosomes and testes rather than ovaries (Rosenthal, 2013). However, a lack of androgen receptors in the bodies of those with AIS causes the development of external genitalia and secondary features typically designated female (e.g., breasts and a vulva) (Rosenthal, 2013). Individuals with guevedoces possess the XY chromosome and testes yet are seemingly born with a vulva. During puberty, however, testosterone is produced at levels that lead to the later development of a penis and scrotum (Rosenthal, 2013). Those with congenital adrenal hyperplasia (CAH) will experience an increase in androgen levels. For individuals classified as female, this increase in androgen levels influences the expression of perceived male attributes (Rosenthal, 2013). Klinefelter's syndrome is one of the most common expressions of chromosomal variance among individuals labeled biologically male at birth (literature notes 0.1–0.2% expression incidence of Klinefelter's syndrome in the general population) (Lanfranco, Kamischke, Zitzmann, & Nieschlag, 2004; Nieschlag, 2013; Rosenthal, 2013; Yarber & Sayad, 2018). Expressing an XXY karyotype on the 23rd chromosome, those with Klinefelter's syndrome often experience hypogonadism (the inability to produce concentrations of testosterone, sperm, or both), gynecomastia (the development of chest colloquially referred to as "man boobs"), and a higher production of follicle-stimulating hormone (FSH), which regulates the production of estrogen and influences a more androgynous presentation in these individuals (Basaria, 2014; Lanfranco, Kamischke, Zitzmann, & Nieschlag, 2004; Nieschlag, 2013; Rosenthal, 2013).

It is not the purpose of this research to ignore the impacts of genetic variance on mortality and quality of life. For example, those with Klinefelter's syndrome, who express an XXY karyotype, have been noted to be at a higher morbidity rate in comparison to those who express an XY karyotype (Rosenthal, 2013; Yarber & Sayad, 2018). Additionally, research shows that those with Klinefelter's syndrome are at higher risk for diseases that include Type II diabetes, embolism, epilepsy, bone fractures, and other physical and mental disorders (although acknowledging this disparity in illness and mortality challenges us to consider whether these higher rates are solely attributable to chromosomal variance or if there is equal accountability surrounding the systemic health education, governance, and care dissemination that is based on a biological sex binary) (Basaria, 2014; Lanfranco, Kamischke, Zitzmann, & Nieschlag, 2004; Nieschlag, 2013). However, the aforementioned examples are used in this context to emphasize that while many promote the belief of a natural binary (i.e., the existence of solely a male–female dichotomy), examples in nature present the argument for sexual and biological fluidity (Basaria, 2014; Lanfranco, Kamischke, Zitzmann, & Nieschlag, 2004; Nieschlag, 2013; Rosenthal, 2013; Yarber & Sayad, 2018). These expressions of variance are scientifically and rigidly regarded as defects, which gives continued insight into the oppressive conceptualizations of normality and abnormality. Further depicting this lens is the way in which biological sex is used as a foundation to classify gender and set the tone for expected gender expression.

What is gender?

Gender is often conflated with biological sex in modern culture. The two are, however, quite different. Gender reflects a sociocultural assignment typically given at birth in which authority figures (i.e., medical professionals, parents, guardians) observe a newborn's external genitalia and decide on which side of the masculine–feminine binary they should live for the remainder of their days (Creighton, 2001; Fausto-Sterling, 2020; Yarber & Sayad, 2018). These authority figures solidify this binary assignment by providing schema-based, gendered, labels such as "boy" and "girl," and engaging in practices such as "discovering the gender of the baby" and hosting gender reveal parties before the child in question is even born. This is only the beginning of an individual's journey with gender. From birth, a person's placement on the gender binary is accompanied by the learning of gender roles, which dictate the perceptions, actions, privileges, and expectations a culture places on an assigned gender (Yarber & Sayad, 2018). Gender assignment is also accompanied by gender stereotypes, which are inflexible beliefs and attitudes one holds about the ways a person assigned to a specific gender should govern themselves (Yarber & Sayad, 2018). Put simply and echoing the sentiments of Hanne Blank (2012), biological sex is used to denote who we are, and gender provides the expectation for what we do and how we should live (Yarber & Sayad, 2018).

It is important to have clear discourse about gender assignment in order to understand that internalized homonegativity, like other concepts regarding sexuality and gender, contain origins that are rooted in fallible constructs. Gender assignment is governed by the chromosomal makeup and external genitalia of a newborn. However, science has revealed that external genitalia is not a fixed marker of identity. Literature highlights the perverse and pervasive nature of the gender binary, as those with ambiguous genitalia are often surgically modified to fit in the spheres of masculinity or femininity (Fausto-Sterling, 2020; Phornphutkul, Boney, Fausto-Sterling, & Gruppuso, 1998). Medical professionals, in collaboration with guardians, psychologists, lawmakers, and other authorities, have also been noted to assign gender based on an individual's perceived reproductive and sexual ability, which is deemed to influence "stable gender identity" (Creighton, 2001; Fausto-Sterling, 2020; Money, Hampson, & Hampson, 1955, 1957; Phornphutkul, Boney, Fausto-Sterling, & Gruppuso, 1998). The idea of stable gender identity stems from Money's (1955, 1957) premise "that children are psychosexually neutral until the age of 2 years and what is required for a stable 'normal' gender identity is unambiguous genitalia and unequivocal assurance from parents as to the chosen gender." While there are some parents and guardians who are becoming resistant to the idea of forcing a specific gender onto a child with ambiguous genitalia, the practice of genitalia normalization surgery remains prevalent (Compton, 2018).

There is danger in this practice, as it supports an ideology in which individuals lack the capacity, or should not have the ability, to identify their own gender—an ideology that has proven to lead some individuals to experience psychological and emotional distress, impaired interpersonal functioning, and death (Money, Hampson, & Hampson, 1955, 1957; Phornphutkul, Boney, Fausto-Sterling, & Gruppuso, 1998). This practice identifies an objective group (e.g., medical professionals, parents, guardians, psychologists) as authorities on gender identity and allows this group to classify individuals as normal and abnormal. Further, one's assigned gender, based on criteria that measures sexual and reproductive functioning, may not be congruent with one's gender identity. Gender identity is described as the way a person internally conceptualizes themselves, their sex, and their being in relation to gender (Yarber & Sayad, 2018). Gender identity speaks to one's internal sense of gender and is a conceptualization that is not visible due to its internal and individual nature. Those for whom their gender identity parallels their gender assignment are typically labeled cisgender, and those who do not identify with the gender they have been assigned at birth are labeled transgender.

In an effort to avoid creating another schema-based binary of cisgender and transgender, which is often used to disseminate privileges and oppressions to the groups commonly perceived as typical and atypical, respectively, it must be emphasized that while transgender is a term that describes those whose gender identity is incongruent with their assigned gender, transgender can also be used as an umbrella term to describe those who are non-binary or those who do not adhere to the gendered scripts that have been expected due to their gender assignment (Yarber & Sayad, 2018). Such nonbinary persons may identify as agender, bigender, genderqueer, genderfluid, or pangender and will transcend the gender binary through gender expression, which includes yet is not limited to dress, hairstyle, bodily characteristics, social engagement, professional pursuit, politics, and use of pronouns (Yarber & Sayad, 2018). Despite social efforts to control and dictate individuals' sex, gender identity, and gender expression, the highlighting of gender-specific and gender-neutral pronouns represent recent actions taken by various advocacy spheres to affirm one's autonomy in determining and expressing their gender identities (Anti-Defamation League; Tobia, 2016; Table 1.1).

For example, if an individual identifies with he/xie pronouns, one may speak of said person in the following manner: "Xie told hir friends about the game he attended last night."

Table 1.1 Gender Pronouns

A nonexhaustive list of pronouns adapted from the Lesbian, Gay, Bisexual, Transgender, Queer, Intersex, Asexual (LGBTQUIA) Resource Center at the University of California, Davis (2019)

___ sang. Talk to ___. That's ___dog. That wallet is ___. Did Jamil stop___?

co	co	cos	cos	coself
en	en	ens	ens	enself
ey	em	eir	eirs	emself
he	him	his	his	himself
she	her	her	hers	herself
they	them	their	theirs	themselves/themselves
xie	hir ("here")	hir	hirs	hirself
ve	vis	vier	ver	verself
yo	yo	yos	yos	yoself

I hope that readers of this work, to this point, are beginning to understand the elusive and fallible natures within the constructs we use to govern our lives and livelihoods. In order to maintain navigation with the use of schemas, which allows us to quickly denote friend and foe, atypical and typical, normal and abnormal, we have ignored the variance that is innate in our being. We have further used this ignorance to argue that the binaries which regulate biological sex and gender can also be applied to sex and sexuality. Such practice only leads to the marginalization and oppression of diverse groups.

Discussing sexuality and gender

Some providers may be reluctant to engage clients in discussions about sexuality and gender due to reasons that range from internal biases to lack of education. The Genderbread diagram (https://www.genderbread.org/) is a great resource that can provide foundational knowledge on biological sex, gender identity and expression, and sexual orientation.

Sexual orientation

Uninduced by biological sex or gender identity is the construct of sexual orientation. The word "uninduced" bears repeating, as many a bigoted person has tried to argue that one's biological sex or assigned gender dictates one's sexual orientation. Sexual orientation is not caused by or correlated with biological sex, gender assignment, or gender identity. Sexual orientation, at its simplest, describes one's sexual and romantic attractions (Rosenthal, 2013; Yarber & Sayad, 2018). I repeat that this definition is presented in its simplest form because there does not seem to be a clear definition of what sexual orientation even is. To be *oriented* to sex and sexuality—thought leaders like Hanne Blank (2012) remind us that this could mean a plethora of things. Is one oriented to engage in sexual intercourse? Does this describe a person who is oriented to possess biological sex? Does this term speak to an individual's personally labeled identity? Or does it depict the identity that has been given to said individual by the sphere(s) in which they interact (Blank, 2012)? There exist many people who have no interest in assuming a label based on who they sexually and romantically engage. There also exist folx who have attempted to force labels onto others based on what they perceive, or have seen, to be an individual's sexual or romantic preference (which we know can change from minute to minute or partner to partner). So, if we cannot achieve a clear understanding of what sexual orientation is, how can we fully give it credibility?

When considering the concept of time, sexual orientation—and the binary presentation of heterosexual versus every other identity—has been recently introduced. According to Hanne Blank's (2012) *Straight: The Surprising Short History of Sexuality*, Angus McLaren's (1997) *The Trials of Masculinity*, and Jonathan Ned Katz's (1995) *The Invention of Heterosexuality*, heterosexuality, homosexuality, and other labels that denote sexual orientation were nonexistent prior to 1868. In fact, the modern labels and understandings of heterosexual and homosexual spring from cultural occurrences that historically highlight social confusions around sexuality, sexuality's place in society, and sexuality's use as a tool to create caste designations. As Blank (2012) describes:

> "Western culture [in the nineteenth century] ... learned to view sexual desire ... as a collection of specific and distinctive desires and activities ... which had a role to play in helping to define a specific and distinctive subtype of human being. Many different desires and acts were given official names in this period ... As these desires and acts were defined and characterized and written down in the right authoritative ways by the right authoritative people, they were used to help create another set of known entities: sexual types. Of these, the most powerful and important, and certainly the most enduring and culture-altering, were 'homosexual' and 'heterosexual.'"

The birth of sexual orientation can be understood through a playful, and incredibly realistic, analogy of adulthood. Every adult who has traversed through life can agree that life is a process of enduring constant transitions with no instruction. For some, such transition may involve pursuing higher education, changing employment, or buying a home. Whatever the situation, each period of transition requires *figuring things out and seeing what works*. Some trials lead to great success, while other trials lead to undesired outcomes. This analogy parallels the social and governmental experiences that led to the construction of sexual orientation.

Hanne Blank's (2012) *Straight: The Surprisingly Short History of Sexuality* suggests that prior to the nineteenth century, labels and clear designations for various sexual acts existed, but there were no explicit designations for sexual orientation or sexual "types" (Beachy, 2010; Blank, 2012; McLaren, 1997; Katz, 1995). However, nineteenth-century legislative and cultural shifts in Europe and the colonized Americas birthed a hypervigilance around sexuality that was directly connected to the reinforcement of social hierarchies and the dissemination and restricting of social privileges.

Blank (2012) describes that in 1866, the formation of modern Germany began as German-speaking kingdoms and territories chose to unify under the Prussian empire. During this formation, leading authorities were tasked with creating legal structures that would complement a new nation—legal structures that built upon the old, religiously influenced, laws that governed sexual matters amongst the previously independent nations. These leaders were experiencing transition and *had to figure out* the laws that would govern sexuality (Blank, 2012). This process influenced the enaction of Paragraph 143 of the Prussian Penal Code of April 14, 1851, which ruled in favor of severe punishment for anyone who was committed of engaging in "unnatural fornication between people and animals, as well as between persons of the male sex" as "such behavior is a demonstration of especial degeneration and degradation of the person and is... dangerous to morality" (Germany & Drage,1885).

Paralleling the governmental changes occurring in Europe was a social argument being made in both Europe and the colonized Western world that called for the preservation of masculinity (Beachy, 2010; Blank, 2012; McLaren, 1997). The colonizers who enslaved inhabitants of other countries, stole land from native peoples in the Americas, and used war and disease to inhabit already occupied spaces believed in a social order that started with a Supreme Deity (i.e., God), and continued with celestial beings and humans (Blank, 2012). Belief in this Great Chain of Order promoted an ideology in which those classed as closest to heavenly enlightenment were white, male, wealthy, physically able, educated, and sexually repressed (Beachy, 2010; Blank, 2012; James, 1902; McLaren, 1997). This zeitgeist, rooted in Darwinism (i.e., a theory of evolution in which certain organisms are better fit to adapt to their environment) and eugenics (i.e., Galton's theory which calls for reproduction in a manner that increases the expression of certain desired qualities in a population), asserted that certain qualities validated and degraded a person's social fitness (Blank, 2012). Although varied sexual expression was once normative, the rising urbanization (and the consequential economic caste shifts) of Europe and the Western colonies caused those of the middle and upper class to associate liberated sexual expression with deviancy, low socioeconomic status, and an inferiority that juxtaposed masculinity and deserved regulation and punishment by law (Blank, 2012; McLaren, 1997; Katz,1995). The rise of, and arguments for, male floggings in Europe and the Americas, as a punishment for sexual crimes during this time, parallel the sentiments of Paragraph 143 of the 1851 Prussian Penal Code and exemplify the ways white, privileged, colonizers systemically initiated the structure of normative and nonnormative sexualities in order to maintain the separation of social and economic castes (Blank, 2012; Germany & Drage, 1885).

The terms "heterosexual" and "homosexual," according to Blank (2012), appeared in schools of thought that were introduced to refute the policing of same-sex sexual attraction. Blank (2012) highlights that upon the introduction of Paragraph 143 of the Prussian Penal Code of 1851, Karl Ulrichs (possibly influenced by his own documented attraction to men and barring from a bureaucratic career once his attraction was discovered) openly opposed this law and argued that same-sex attraction was naturally innate and unable to be changed. Having been exposed to medical literature around hermaphrodites (commonly known now as intersex individuals), Ulrichs—through a series of self-published pamphlets in 1864—asserted the idea of same-sex attraction being a form of hermaphroditism—or "sexual inversion"—in which the *Urning* (a man who loves other men) possessed a male physical body yet a female mind (Blank, 2012; Stack, 2020).

Opposing Ulrich's suggestion of same-sex attracted men having a female psyche, Karl Maria Kertbeny argued that same-sex attracted men did not differ in their masculinity and overall contribution to society and should therefore be awarded complete legal and social citizenship (Blank, 2012; Stack, 2020). While there is no evidence identifying Kertbeny as same-sex attracted, account is taken of the way he witnessed the blackmailing of his same-sex attracted male peers for their "abnormal tastes." Kertbeny, like Ulrich's, outwardly opposed Paragraph 143 of the Prussian Penal code of 1851; and in written correspondence with Ulrichs in 1868, Kertbeny introduced the idea of "homosexuals" being parallel and equal to "heterosexuals" (Blank, 2012; Stack, 2020). However, the terms "heterosexual" and "homosexual" were slow to develop traction and were not recognized as independent from biological sex and gender (the distinctions between biological sex, gender, and sexual orientation began to appear in the latter half of the 1900s).

It was in 1886 that the term "heterosexual" became popularized in *Psychopathia Sexualis* by Austro-German psychiatrist and sexologist Richard von Krafft-Ebing (whose conservative views around sexuality were parallel to that of the Catholic church) (Blank, 2012). Yet this work, which was intended to assist legislators in ruling cases around sexual misconduct, not only inadvertently highlighted the term "heterosexual." Krafft-Ebing's interchangeable use of heterosexual and "normal sexuality" sewed religious seeds of thought that positioned opposite gendered sexual intercourse, within marriage, for the purpose of procreation as the only natural form of sex; while every other form of sexual expression became situated as "crimes against nature" (Krafft-Ebing, 1926). These "crimes against nature" included, but were not limited to, sadism, masochism, thinking too much about sex, and having too little sexual desire; and further highlight the efforts to classify sexuality that is normative and nonnormative in order to disseminate and restrict social privileges (Krafft-Ebing, 1926).

Robert Beachy (2010), in his exploration of the ways Germany set the foundation for the introduction and conceptualization of labels defining sexual orientation, supports Blanks historical account and provides a more in-depth history of the etiology of the homosexual label. According to Beachy (2010), the efforts of the German-state authorities (including Prussia) to maintain and enhance anti-sodomy laws contrasted with the progressive movements of surrounding nations influenced by the reforms of the French Revolution (states such as Spain, Italy, the Netherlands, and Belgium decriminalized same gender sexual engagement and "exempted same gender sexual acts from criminal prosecution except in cases of the application of force or with children"). Beachy (2010) details the ways in which Paragraph 143 eventually evolved to become Paragraph 175 of Germany's Imperial Criminal Code, which defined sodomy as sexual acts between two men and between man and beast. What stands interesting is that Paragraph 175 of Germany's Imperial Code was enacted by a conservative government despite the protests of medical professionals and scientists who emphasized the lack of evidence to support the perception of the difference between opposite gender and same gender attracted individuals (Beachy, 2010). In irradicating the highest courts in its territories, the German Supreme Court further expanded Paragraph 175 to criminalize the punishment of all sex acts that were interpreted to contrast heterosexual sex (Beachy, 2010). This expansion positioned various sex acts to be seen as perversions and manifestations of mental illness. The criminalization of sodomy additionally justified the stripping of privilege from those who engaged in same-sex love. This expansion was accompanied by a counterargument to "sexual inversion" (made by Krafft-Ebings and supported by some scientific and medical leaders) to emphasize the perverse nature of same-sex attraction and sexual engagement (Beachy, 2010).

However, Beachy (2010) notes that despite the presence of Paragraph 175, there were individuals who opposed the legislative oppression of those who participated in same-sex sexual engagement. He presents the way in which Ulrich's, during a time of same-sex criminalization, coined the terms *Urning* (describing men who are sexually and romantically attracted to men) and *Urninden* (denoting women who are sexually and romantically attracted to women); exposed himself as an *Urning*; and advocated against the Prussian anti-sodomy statute (Beachy, 2010). In addition to Ulrich's role of advocate, Beachy (2010) highlights that Krafft-Ebings' views on sexuality, which were once influenced by religion and prejudice against same-sex attracted folx, became more progressive as he used research and case study narratives of same-sex attracted men, in *Psychopathia Sexualis,* to continue Ulrich's advocacy against Paragraph 175 in medical and lay spaces (Beachy, 2010; Krafft-Ebings, 1926). Beachy (2010) adds that in Krafft-Ebings' last publication on the theory of sexual inversion, he renounced his theory against sexual inversion and stated that homosexuality "should not be viewed as a psychic depravity or even sickness."

Regardless of the historical account, it can be agreed that the initial labels for sexual orientation (i.e., heterosexual and homosexual) have their origins in a conservatism that sought to define and differentiate the socially normal from the abnormal. One can observe a pattern (rooted in the fundamental idea of the Great Chain of Order) in which one group (or in the case of white supremacy, many groups) must be oppressed for another group to be positioned as superior and powerful (Beachy, 2010; Blank, 2012). The process which birthed the labels *heterosexual* and *homosexual* highlights a history in which the desire to preserve power among one group justified oppression and inequity based on gender, sex, and sexuality.

What's your truth?

• What have been the messages you've received about biological sex, gender, gender expression, and sexual orientation?

An additional (possibly annoying) aside on biological sex, gender, and sexual orientation

Efforts have been taken to present information on biological sex, gender assignment, gender identity, gender expression, and sexual orientation to only highlight that these experiences—these constructs—*are not real* and are rooted in *presentation* and *performativity* (Butler, 1988; Jagger, 2008).

Yes, one's biological sex and genetic composition are workings that have roots in science. However, there is no monolithic or rigidly typical presentation of this biological makeup (in fact, hormone and reproductive output are so variant that scientific and medical authorities commonly argue for ranges of normalcy) (Rosenthal, 2013). When one considers the prevalence of biological variance that occurs in humans over time (e.g., biological shifts that are present at birth, changes that occur in puberty, developments with aging, and nuances that appear in response to the environment, circumstance, or medication), the biological binary is further challenged (Rosenthal, 2013). Arguments have asserted that the performance of gender roles and "normative" sexuality must exist for the population to continue (Money, Hampson, & Hampson, 1955; Money, Hampson, & Hampson, 1957). However, numerous examples highlight that those expansive in their gender and sexuality have no bearing upon the furthering of humanity. Gender variant individuals produce biological children; and those unable to produce biological children through sexual engagement have been able to successfully reproduce with scientific advancement (Yarber & Sayad, 2018). Further, those who perform heterosexuality and adhere to traditional gender and sexuality scripts have historically expressed fluidity through acts such as producing progeny and simultaneously engaging in same gender loving sexual or romantic interactions throughout their lifespans (Kinsey, 1948, 1953).

Sex, gender, and sexuality are fluid and vary from individual to individual. No authority figure, government official, family member, or external source has the power to place a person on a binary or define who that person is. However, adherence to the gender binary has historically been used to dictate how individuals navigate through the world, and to reward and punish those who follow and deviate from the scripts given by their gender assignment. The incorporation of race, religion, socioeconomic status, age, ability status, and other variables further complicate the dissemination of gender- and sexuality-based privilege, as gendered scripts (i.e., masculine performance) are often caricatured through the lens of Eurocentric/white supremacist standards (Blank, 2012; Collins, 2004; Collins & Bilge, 2020; hooks, 2004). This lens has aided in the implementation of distorted truths around gender performance—what one can wear, how one must behave, and to whom one must be sexually and romantically attracted—which cements race-. wealth-, age-, ability-, and other-diversity-variable-based molds of masculinity that position whiteness and white masculinity as socially superior.

Refocusing on sexual orientation

Commonly accepted social beliefs and behaviors around sexual orientation have seemingly evolved since the nineteenth century. In countries throughout the world, same-sex sexual engagement has been decriminalized, particularly in most majority white populated territories (a phenomenon to be visited later in this work). In the United States, the 2015 outcome of *Obergefell v. Hodges* ruled that "state bans on same-sex marriage and on recognizing same-sex marriages duly performed in other jurisdictions are unconstitutional under the due process and equal protection clauses of the 14th Amendment to the U.S. Constitution" (Obergefell v. Hodges, 2015). In 2020, the U.S. Supreme Court supported further social protections for individuals expansive in their gender and sexual identities when it ruled that the Civil Rights Act of 1964, which forbade workplace discrimination based on sex, should be extended to include workplace discrimination based on sexual orientation and gender identity (Liptak, 2020). Contrasting the experience of Karl Ulrichs, who lived when same-sex attraction could hinder one's social and occupational trajectory, there has occurred a recent increase in the amount of openly same-sex attracted persons—such as United States Representatives Mondaire Jones and Ritchie Torres, American film director Lee Daniels, actor Coleman Domingo, singer MNEK, and rappers Lil Nas X, Karnage Kills, and Cakes Da Killa—who exist in spheres of influence.

Further highlighting the current culture of sexuality and sexual orientation acceptance, individuals are moving beyond the rigid labels of heterosexual and homosexual and are expanding their vocabulary to capture diversity within sexual orientation (Donaghue, 2015). Identities such as queer (a word once used to discriminate, now reclaimed and transformed to describe one who does not identify with heterosexuality or cisgender identity), bisexual (a term used to describe one sexually and/or romantically attracted to more than one gender) pansexual/"pan" (a term denoting one who possesses sexual and/or romantic attraction regardless of one's biological sex or gender identity), demisexual/"demi" (a term used to describe one whose sexual expression is contingent upon a strong emotional and personal connection, rather than on physical appearance or sexual desire), and asexual/ace (used to describe who with no or low levels of sexual desire, despite their possible proclivity toward romantic engagement) depict an evolution in the understanding and acceptance of sexual and romantic orientations that have always existed (Grant & Francis, 2021; OUT Right Action International, 2020). The propagation of these labels further challenges the binary understanding of sexuality that is used to afford and restrict privileges—a binary understanding which institutes social castes that distinguish the enlightened from the base (Blank, 2012; Fausto-Sterling, 2020; Foucault, 2012). Yet amid this progress, some individuals with expansive sexual orientations continue to oppress themselves and others in their communities.

The white supremacist ideals that have historically been used to marginalize those who transcend the qualities associated with Eurocentric puritanism have, over time, become internalized and used as a tool to assist non- "mainstream" groups in perpetuation of their own marginalization (Collins, 2004; hooks, 2004; Lemelle, 2010). Folx who have been historically subjugated have learned to continue the tactics of their oppressors. This inheritance sustains transphobia, and its life-threatening consequences, in genderqueer communities; it keeps Black women in a social cycle that volleys them between the role of expected savior and disrespected social mule; and it keeps many Black same gender loving men in a space of internalized homonegativity, in which they constantly weigh the costs and benefits of embracing or repressing their sexual and romantic attractions.

Internalized homonegativity is ...

Hating yourself for being gay.

Avery, 33, Washington, D.C.

2 Internalized Homonegativity and Same Gender Loving Black Men

Like the tendency of individuals to incorrectly label themselves "not racist," many folx believe—and often publicly profess—that they are not homonegative. The denial of homonegativity in society is often supported by literature that highlights the ever-growing approval of same-gender unions, the increase in support for coming out, the rise in same gender loving social protections, and the increased representation of same gender loving people in politics, entertainment, religion, and others spheres that once rejected same gender loving presence (Encyclopedia Britannica, 2020; Faderman, 2016; George Mason University; Liptak, 2020). However, although homonegativity may be harder to identify in a society which prides itself on social progress, homonegativity and its often-life-threatening consequences are still explicitly and implicitly present in communities that have been marginalized and subordinated by the majority culture.

Truth: Homonegativity toward same gender loving Black men appears in various forms

In 2012, the alleged "death by hazing" of Florida A&M University band drum major Robert Champion was scrutinized because of his openly gay identity (Munzenrieder, 2012). Since expressing his enjoyment of receiving analingus (or rimming) in 2016, the topic of singer Tank's sexual and romantic identities has been frequently discussed by the public (Ransom, 2019). Famed entertainer, Billy Porter, has frequently called for a reformation of the homonegativity he perceives to pervade the Black community (Assunção, 2020). These examples provide a small glimpse into homonegativity's impact on Black men. Homonegativity causes lifelong trauma; it inhibits sexual exploration;

DOI: 10.4324/9781003180937-3

it can lead to death. Prominent Black figures, such as Al Shapton, have argued that the Black community is not inherently homonegative. This concept, to be explored in later chapters, is valid. The Black community has a longstanding history of being focused on the preservation and upliftment of all its members (Ward, 2005; Winder, 2015). The Black community has also been heavily indoctrinated in a homonegative conditioning that is rooted in a seemingly desperate social effort to preserve a distorted image of Black masculinity that has been constructed and measured by white supremacy and white masculinity (Collins, 2006; hooks, 2004; Lemelle, 2010). This is clearly demonstrated in the way same gender loving female identities, through manipulation by the male gaze, are placed on a social dichotomy of hypersexuality or fraternized invisibility, yet Black male same gender loving identities are presented as controversial in many conservative and progressive Black spaces (Grant, 2020b; hooks, 2004; Richardson, 2011; Smyth, 1990). Homonegativity toward Black men has become so pervasive that the conceptualization of same gender loving status often expands beyond romantic and sexual attraction to include behavioral expression (Grant, 2020b; hooks, 2004; Johnson, 2014).

An example of homonegativity in progressive sphere arises through *Whoreible Decisions*, a podcast led by two Black women, Weezy and Mandi, who enjoy sex, seek to expand their sexual horizons, and use lived experiences to encourage the general public in expanding their sexual tastes. Since the show's inception, viewers have watched the hosts navigate their sexual and romantic identities and the sexual and romantic identities of their various partners. In this navigation has arisen noteworthy disclosures from Mandi, who proudly expressed her proclivity and pleasure for pegging (i.e., the act of penetrating a cisgender, oftentimes heterosexual, man in the anus) Black men (The Black Effect). Although data highlights the countless men who enjoy receptive anal penetration through pegging, since Mandi's disclosure, she has often endured homonegative responses, has felt compelled to defend the heterosexuality of her partners, and has engaged in the labor of teaching various men and women that Black men engaging in, and receiving pleasure from, anal stimulation does not denote the same gender loving identity (The Black Effect). This example highlights that when applied to Black male sexuality, homonegativity does not just expand beyond Herek's (2015) description of negative attitudes toward same gender loving identity and behavior. The rigid rules around sexuality and masculine performance, rooted in homonegativity, often enforce limitations on sexual expression in heterosexual sexual engagement.

The Pour Minds Podcast stands as another sexuality-based podcast that is gaining increased traction in the Black community. Hosted by two Black women who share the ins and outs of acquiring, dating, and disposing of rich men, these women often review various male behaviors (e.g., a man's mannerisms, whether he enjoys anal penetrations with multiple fingers, how he positions himself to receive analingus, etc.) and assess whether these behaviors can "make a man gay" (Apple Podcasts). As reflected by the public response to singer Tank's sexual desires and engagements—revealed on popular, Black-targeted, media shows such as *The Breakfast Club* and *Angela Yee's Lip Service*—there seem to be specific behaviors that are commonly conceptualized by some members of the Black community as actions exclusively performed by same gender loving men. Further, there exists an inflexible manner of thinking that delineates men who have experimented with men, or who enjoy anal play, as undesirable to women seeking relationships with men. Arguments such as, "I don't want to have to compete with men *and* women" or "that's just my preference" have been often used to shroud the homonegativity that fuels such perspectives and preferences (Apple Podcasts). However, these excuses further highlight the homonegative thinking that is embedded in the Black community, which targets and limits varied expressions of Black manhood, Black male sexuality, and Black male sexual fulfillment.

Now, homonegativity in the Black community doesn't just impact Black male sexual and romantic fulfillment. There currently exists real, life and death, consequences of homonegativity for Black men and boys. To repeat, homonegativity physically and spiritually kills Black men and boys (Assunção, 2020; Munzenrieder, 2012). Homonegativity has led to Black men and boys being rejected from homes, disfranchised, mentally and emotionally scarred, and susceptible to the ensnarement of physical, mental, emotional, and sexual predators (Icard, et al., 2020; Marshall, Shannon, Kerr, Zhang, & Wood, 2010; Martinez, 2020; United States Department of Justice, 2020). Brief mention must acknowledge the Black same gender loving men who have died by overdose while engaged with politician Ed Buck, who was exposed in 2017 for his alleged kinks related to drugging and sexually assaulting Black men (United States Department of Justice, 2020). These were men living with addiction, who had been of stripped social and other supports, allegedly due to their sexual identities. These were also men who represent countless unidentified same gender loving

Black men whose disenfranchisement and abuse have gone un-acknowledged. Homonegativity toward Black men is a current and serious issue with current and serious consequences.

What's your truth?

- What are your thoughts about internalized homonegativity?
- How have you engaged with, or experienced, internalized homo-negativity?
- What are some behaviors you have been told Black men should not engage, lest they be labeled same gender loving?
- How have these messages limited your experiences, or the experiences of Black men you know?
- In your opinion, how do these rigid rules around behavior impact Black men?

Truth: Everyone has experiences with homonegativity … and yet homonegativity not the real issue

Everyone whose lives have been shaped in a capitalistic, white supre-macist, patriarchal society will, at some point throughout their life-span, engage with homonegativity—as one who both perpetuates and internalizes homonegativity. I have internalized homonegativity. You have internalized homonegativity. It is the inheritance we have re-ceived by being indoctrinated in an environment that is fueled by systemic oppression. Herek (2015) highlights that the internalization of homonegativity can be experienced by heterosexuals and same gender loving folx alike. Internalized homonegativity influences the propa-gation of behaviorally based judgments that reinforce the endorsing of rigid differentiation between heterosexual and same gender loving identities and practices (Herek, 2015). While these differentiations are often not based on fact and credibility, many people have chosen to believe themselves to possess an internal sense (i.e., a "gaydar") in which they can identify same gender loving people—specifically, same gender loving men—based on behavioral practices or gender expres-sions (hooks, 2004; Pascoe, 2011; Stoller, 1990). This assumptive way of living has prompted many men—heterosexual and same gender loving—to become hypervigilant of the ways they show up in various spheres (Grant 2020; hooks, 2004; Lemelle, 2010). This hypervigilance has also influenced many men to highlight and regulate the assumingly same gender loving presentations and behaviors of other men in order to reduce the attention garnered by their own actions and expressions (hooks, 2004; Pascoe, 2011). This pattern of practice has become a salient phenomenon among Black men, as evidenced by eras in which colloquialisms such as "pause" became popular. Like the declaration of "no homo" in majority culture, Black men would exclaim "pause" after making a statement (i.e., "I love you, man") or engaging in a behavior (i.e., hugging or wrestling a man) that seemed to communicate homoeroticism or position them in a perceived same gender loving manner. Such social patterns have amplified experiences of distress in many Black same gender loving men, who then become convinced that they must make effort to hide any socially regarded inklings of same gender loving affiliations (Grant, 2020b; Collins, 2006; hooks, 2004). These men often navigate a dialectic of protecting and dishonoring themselves and their identities while traversing homonegative environments.

In scrutinizing the homonegative experiences of Black men, internalized homonegativity does not solely relate to sexual orientation and identity disclosure, as often depicted by mainstream culture. My dissertation qualitatively explored the ways Black men navigated internalized homonegativity. In this study, one participant candidly processed the experiences associated with being same gender loving and gaining comfort with one's sexual and romantic orientations. He profoundly asked whether "[internalized homonegativity] is really the issue at hand" (Grant, 2020b). This participant highlighted the possibility that "if [he came] out, [he may not] conquer homonegativity" (Grant, 2020b). This observation acknowledges that while Herek may have provided a stable foundational premise of internalized homonegativity, the issue of internalized homonegativity for Black men expands beyond the scopes of sexual and romantic desire and identity acceptance.

3 Constructing Black Manhood: Homonegativity, Hegemonic Masculinity, and Femmephobia

My indoctrination into homonegativity did not come from communication that same gender loving identity was immoral or socially incorrect. My introduction to homonegativity was tied to behaviorally based characterization from my community—characterizations that labeled me "sweet". In my first experience with an all-Black summer day camp, I become known as "sweet boy" due to my minimal interest in sports and high interest in Sailor Moon, playing with girls, and gossip. Fellow Black schoolboys often stopped me in the lonely hallways of our greater Philadelphia private school to remind me that I was "sweet." Adult church members of my predominantly Caribbean religious institution often noticed my detail-oriented ways of approaching tasks and would condescendingly observe that I was "sweet" in the ways I navigated. As a child, I had no idea what "sweet" described, yet this reoccurring label had a significant impact on my psyche and social navigation. I can remember playing at an afterschool program and spontaneously exclaiming to one of the caregivers that "I [wasn't] sweet" to which said caregiver asked, "Why did you say that?"

Why did I say that? What meanings did I associate with the word "sweet" as I developed my Black male identity? And what themes do these engagements with my environment communicate regarding the making of Black boyhood and manhood in a white supremacist society?

> I depended on my brother to figure out how my mannerisms should be. How I talked, the accents I made on certain words, or how I walked, or how I would carry my bookbag. Those small things are notes I picked up from my brother in order to act masculine to get by in the community I lived in so I wouldn't be attacked with the words "faggot" or "gay."
>
> Rammy, 30, Wilson, NC

DOI: 10.4324/9781003180937-4

Truth: Homonegativity is inextricably linked to hegemonic masculinity

The beginning of this work introduced homonegativity as negative attitudes toward same gender loving individuals and same gender loving behavior. It is interesting to note, however, that anti-same gender loving attitudes, at their core, are rarely ever directly targeted toward same gender loving people or same gender loving behaviors (Herek, 2015). So often, one can observe this phenomenon being ex-emplified through the ways folx profess their love for same gender loving people yet emphasize their "disagreement" with the idea of same gender lovingness. This is further replicated in the perceptions of same gender loving Black men. While completing my dissertation research with this cohort, I found that none of the men were uncomfortable with sexually or romantically engaging with other men. The discomfort with their same gender loving status was rooted in a conditioned perception that same gender loving identity somehow challenged their status, and accompanying privileges, as men (Grant, 2020). Heterosexism—a term previously introduced in this work—is understood to be the systemic, cultural, social, and individual ideology that normalizes and privileges heterosexuality, and abnormalizes, marginalizes, and disenfranchises non-heterosexual sexualities (Szymanski, Kashubeck-West, & Meyer, 2008). While heterosexism speaks to the general systemic oppression of lesbian, gay, bisexual, and other sexualities, heterosexism does not fully account for the homo-negativity felt by the Black men, interviewed in my dissertation, toward their sexualities. Heterosexism does not fully account for my interesting relationship with the word "sweet". Heterosexism also does not fully account for the multifaceted risks Black men perceive to accompany same gender loving identity, identity disclosure, behavioral expression, or communal affiliation.

Hegemonic masculinity serves as the moderating link between heterosexism and homonegativity among heterosexual and same gender loving Black men. Oversimplified, hegemony involves the practice of one group asserting their dominance over another group (Buchbinder, 2013; Connell & Messerschmidt, 2005). This is observed through the historical practices of colonialism, the implementation of caste structures, and the reinforcing of social mores that strengthen the deli-neation between the privileged and the oppressed (Blank, 2012). However, hegemony does not only involve the practice of one group's domination over another. What makes hegemony so strikingly per-vasive is its ability to empower and privilege one group, while convincing those of the oppressed group that the dichotomy of privileged and marginalized—and this dichotomy's accompanying attitudes, emotions, behaviors, and social structures—is normative and appropriate. The dominating practice of hegemony cannot thrive without the oppressed who believe in, cosign, and reinforce their oppression. From this logic, there therefore cannot exist a socially limiting belief of heterosexuality being the norm if there are not heterosexual and same gender loving folx who endorse this belief through their negative attitudes toward same gender loving identity and behavior (Buchbinder, 2013; Connell & Messerschmidt, 2005; Pascoe, 2011).

Now that we understand hegemony as a practice of dominance, hegemonic masculinity describes an idealized, caricatured, presentation of masculinity that often emphasizes white manhood, physical and sexual prowess, financial prosperity, and emotional toughness. Some researchers present hegemonic masculinity through the narrow lens of relationships between men and women (Connell, 1987; Connell & Messerschmidt, 2005; Pascoe, 2011); yet as gender and gender expression transcend the male–female binary, hegemonic masculinity can be more accurately understood through the relationship between masculinities and femininities. Hegemonic masculinity is a hyperbolized presentation of masculinity that has been used to historically justify white, cisgender, masculine dominance over femininities and non-white masculinities. Through this justification, hegemonic masculinity has also been used as a socially accepted standard to secure a gender order of masculinity over femininity, and denote the types of masculinities that should be privileged and marginalized, based on their proximity to femininity.

Connell (1987) reminds us that the dominance of a specific form of masculinity over other masculinities and femininities is not "achieved at the point of the gun, or by threat of unemployment," but "[this] ascendency is embedded in religious doctrine and practice, mass media content, wage structures, the design of housing, welfare/taxation policies and so forth" (p. 184). This is reflected in same gender loving communities, as the masculine ideal is revered through the correlation of expressed masculinity (usually in the form of extreme physical fitness, stereotypically masculine dress, and penetrative sexual positioning) with perceived desirability; through the placement of perceivably feminine same gender loving men on the social margins; and through the ways many same gender loving men describe in their personal narratives of experienced homonegativity a hypervigilance of, and aversion to, behaviors that could be coded as feminine (Anderson, 2005; Connell, 1987; Connell & Messerschmidt, 2005; Grant 2020a, 2020b; Hale & Ojeda, 2018; Pascoe, 2011). This relationship with hegemonic masculinity communicates that there exist specific standards of masculinity men must meet in order to receive social privileges (standards rooted in being white, able-bodied/physically strong, logical rather than emotional, inhabiting a role of "protector and provider" etc.). The idealized "real man" is a trope that many men become introduced to, indoctrinated within, and encouraged to follow from the early stages of boyhood (Connell & Messerschmidt, 2005; Hale & Ojeda, 2018; Pascoe, 2011). The indoctrination of this trope can explain why some men experience internalized homonegativity when their sexual identities become the subject of public discussion. The experienced homonegativity does not explicitly relate to the protentional uncovering of a man's same gender loving sexual and romantic attractions. The homonegativity, however, responds to the environmental suggestion that the man in question possesses or exudes traits that are socially coded as non-masculine.

> When I think about folx that say they're tops, I think internalized homonegativity automatically correlates top to being masculine, and if you're a feminine top, that's shunned. And vice versa, if you're a masculine Bottom, or a heavier Bottom, or a taller Bottom, I think homonegativity shames that person. Personally, I still struggle with appearance and being a gay man. There's this extra pressure to be super fit and, for me, not being fit adds an extra layer of negative thoughts.
>
> Chris, 30, Charlotte, NC

There may be some who disagree with the pervasive nature of hegemonic masculinity in present society, as cultural shifts have allowed for increasingly diverse presentations of masculinity. Of course, manhood in the twenty-first century has evolved to which many men are allowed to be more emotionally available and focused on personal connection over financial domination; and are able to express an expansive range of thoughts, emotions, and behaviors that deviate from rigid masculine mores. Morrow (2000), however, reminds us that hegemonic masculinity is an exaggerated form of masculinity that changes in presentation as societies and cultures change. Morrow (2000) additionally notes that while no man can ever fully achieve the established standard of hegemonic masculinity, hegemonic masculinity continues to thrive because it exists as a form of masculinity many men believe in (remember, hegemony cannot oppress without the belief of the oppressed in their oppression) and, in various ways, seek to enact. Despite the acceptance of male diversity in qualities such as emotion, physical frame, style of dress and socioeconomic standing, hegemonic masculinity has become so ingrained in the social belief system that it is able to adapt to social changes and remain the endorsed belief of many men and women.

Connell (1995) expands the understanding of hegemonic masculinity by presenting various forms of masculinity men may engage. Connell (1995) notes that *complicit masculinity* depicts men who disengage from the practice of hegemonic masculinity yet benefit from hegemonic masculine social mores. This form of masculinity may be engaged by men who are emotionally available and inadherent to scripts of toughness and physical prowess, yet who may also be uninclined to shift the systems (i.e., the social standards of hegemonic masculinity) that place these men in a dominant social caste. These are the men who may have same gender loving friends and may traverse same gender loving spaces, yet may not object to the heterosexist and homonegative views that arise when they are engaged with their heterosexual peers. Connell (1995) uses *subordinated masculinity* to describe those who are often socially disenfranchised by the ways they do not fit the rigid norms of hegemonic masculinity. This classification may include same gender loving men who are positioned as socially subordinate to their heterosexual counterparts. This category also includes same gender loving men who are further categorized into spheres of femininity based on factors such as their physique or their inconsistent performance of masculinity (i.e., fats and femmes). Connell (1995) also identifies *marginalized masculinities* to describe men who receive privileges due to their positions as biological men, yet are disenfranchised based on factors such as race or class. This category includes men of color, men of low socioeconomic status, or men who may be diverse in disability status, age, or religious affiliation. Understanding these additional masculinities transforms hegemonic masculinity from a praxis to a position men may inhabit regardless of whether they adhere to the scripts and practices of traditional hegemony.

When hegemonic and accompanying masculinities are applied to the lived context of Black heterosexual and same gender loving men, an interesting phenomenon arises in which socially subordinated and marginalized masculinities strive toward the idealized form of masculinity and disenfranchise presentations that do not align with this pursuit (Connell 1995; Dean, 2013). It is here we observe the trickle-down categorization and marginalization of the sweet boys, fats, and femmes in the Black community. Black men will never reach the ideal of white hegemonic masculinity. They are privileged due to their manhood but marginalized due to their race; yet the belief Black men have in patriarchal power and dominance justifies their subordination of same gender loving Black masculinities. Further, the belief Black same gender loving men have in the power and privilege of masculinity incites internalized homonegativity and aids in the maintenance of hegemonic masculinity through acts such as the social and sociopolitical ostracization of same gender loving men who do not adhere to hegemonic masculine scripts.

> A Black man is supposed to like women. A Black man isn't supposed to be gay. A Black man is supposed to be tough.
>
> Justin, 30, Cleveland, OH

Truth: Hegemonic masculinity cannot thrive without femmephobia

In addition to promoting an exaggerated form of masculine performance, hegemonic masculinity requires effortful separation from associations with femininity and aggressive dominance over that which is feminine. Femmephobia describes prejudice toward femininity and feminine expressions and makes the rejection of femininity and feminine expression a social value. In many Judeo-Christian spaces, femininity has been consistently denigrated through depictions of women. Eve has been biblically positioned as physically subordinate to Adam, due to being fashioned from his rib, and has been made responsible for the fall of humanity; Delilah has been used to depict the deceptive nature of femininity which must be resisted; Jezebel has been used by patriarchal influences to present femininity and womanhood as sexually unstable, perverse, and in need of patriarchal control (Buchbinder, 2013). Femmephobia and hegemonic masculinity are identified in secular culture through the institutional and cultural practices against women and femmes, which include unequal wages, physical and sexual assault, and intimate partner violence (Hale & Ojeda, 2018; Hoskin, 2019). According to the extant literature, femmephobia is a foundational trait that creates room for the experience of internalized homonegativity among Black same gender loving men (hooks, 2004; Lemelle, 2010; Dean, 2013). Before identifying same gender sexual and romantic attractions, many Black same gender loving men identify themselves, or are identified by others, as exhibiting behaviors that are commonly coded as feminine. These characterizations range from having interests in academics over sports, to being emotionally expressive, to having more female than male friends, to simply existing in a male-dominated space while holding perceivably feminine physical posturing (Hale & Ojeda, 2018; Pascoe, 2011; Slatton & Spates, 2014; 2016).

Hegemonic masculinity teaches same gender loving Black boys and men that their presentations—their beings—align with femininity and do not meet the hegemonically masculine ideal; they are marginalized by race and subordinated by sexual and romantic attraction. In order to meet hegemonic standards, same gender loving Black men and boys are conditioned by various environments to separate themselves from femininity, as much as possible, and assert their dominance over femininity in order to place themselves higher on the hierarchy of masculine identities (Boykin & Shange, 2012; Grant, 2020; hooks, 2004). Such efforts can be emotionally, mentally, and interpersonally taxing, as the pursuit of the hegemonic masculinity strips Black same gender loving men from embracing their identities and cultivating relationships that facilitate a greater understanding of self and others. These efforts further reinforce the idea that manhood (and consequently, Black manhood) can be measured on a masculine-feminine binary that further distorts Black male sense of self and increases the distress Black same gender loving men experience regarding their sexual and romantic identities (Buchbinder, 2013; Connell, 1987, 1995; Connell & Meserschmidt, 2005; Grant, 2020; hooks, 2004).

We see it in media

Research details the power of representation in media. Folx, diverse in race and cultural background, who can see themselves represented in media often experience an expansion in the perceptions they possess of their lived possibilities (Caswell, Migoni, Geraci, & Cifor, 2017; GLAAD, 2019; Smith, Choueiti, & Pieper, 2016). With this considered, one must be critically curious about the limited portrayals of Black same gender loving men in digital media. The Black same gender loving men interviewed in my dissertation identified that a part of their identity confusion stemmed from not witnessing themselves represented in media (Grant, 2020b). Black same gender loving men are usually portrayed on a rigid binary of caricatured masculinity or femininity. They are either represented by the thuggish, down low, hardened portrayals of Omar Little in *The Wire*, Chiron in *Moonlight,* and Lil Murda in *P Valley*; or by the sassy, church mother-esque, almost mammy-like, flamboyant characterizations of Titus in *Unbreakable Kimmy Schmidt* and Pray Tell in *Pose*. There currently exists no television media outlet that highlights the diversity and nuance among Black same gender loving men.

What's your truth?

• What have been the common depictions of Black same gender loving men, and Black same gender loving male life, you've witnessed, in media, throughout your lifespan? How have these depictions impacted your assumptions of, biases toward, or engagements with same gender loving Black men?

In 2005, director Patrick Ian Polk (a Black SGL man) sought to challenge the monolithic portrayal of same gender loving Black men with his television series *Noah's Arc*. Perceived by many to be the "Black gay *Sex and the City*," *Noah's Arc* challenged the masc-femme binary zeitgeist by offering audiences Black same gender loving characters who represented various cultures within the Black same gender loving community. Noah represented the femme boys, Alex represented the butch queens, Chance channeled the intellectual Black same gender loving man, and Ricky represented the empowered, gym-going, socialite. Other characters on *Noah's Arc* expanded Black same gender loving representation by highlighting same gender loving men who were religious, in medicine, in entertainment, and on the down low. Polk's television series so adequately captured the diversity among Black same gender loving men that *Noah's Arc* served (and still serves) as an integral coming-of-age medium for many Black same gender loving men. Unfortunately, this television series was discontinued after a year's run. Since *Noah's Arc*, multifaceted depictions of Black same gender loving men have yet to be seen on television again.

When the narrative is controlled by Black same gender loving men, those are very positive and I very much love those representations. When the narrative isn't as controlled from that group, there's still this very negative thing that is only reduced to sex, the body—this sort of gravitational pull toward sex and the body. I feel like when I see same gender loving Black men, or those who I assume to be, it's always this hypersexualized display of asses, penises, chests—all these things that I think, at least temporarily, deny me, and I would say all of us, from the pleasure of having more robust and expansive community that aren't limited to the body.

Simeon, 31, Brooklyn, NY

In media we're stereotyped and fetishized. There's not a show on television that shows Black gay men as everyday people. Even though it's more accepted, the presentation is still stereotyped— very femme, queenie; and there's nothing wrong with that, but that's just one type of same gender loving Black gay men. There're all kinds of types.

Avery, 33, Washington, D.C.

The erasure of the nuanced and multifaceted representation found in *Noah's Arc* speaks to the pervasive and persistent nature of hegemonic masculinity in society. Hegemonic masculinity positions Black same gender loving men as marginalized and subordinated within the hierarchies of masculinity. Hegemonic masculinity also reinforces this positioning by conditioning Black same gender loving men to maintain patriarchal dominance through adherence to a masculine-feminine performance binary. Despite the cultural shifts that allow white masculinities the privilege of expanding what constitutes masculinity, Black same gender loving men have been stripped of representations that reinforce the diversity within the Black same gender loving community; they have been confined to spheres that rigidly classify one as feminine butch queen or down-low masculine thug. These strict categorizations lay the foundation for experienced identity confusion in men who may not fully align with such presentations. The resultant identity confusion then leads to internalized homonegativity, for if one cannot see their unique presentation represented in media or their external world, one may begin to believe that one's being is unnatural, atypical, and worthy of denigration.

We see it in social navigation

The theme of hegemonic masculinity's influence on men to separate themselves from femininity is further highlighted in the observed relationship between some Black same gender loving men and Black transgender women. My research and clinical practice have allowed me to interact with various Black same gender loving men who, at some point in our exploration of their sexual and romantic attractions, have expressed discomfort toward Black transgender women. What stands interesting is that many of these men have coded their discomfort as internalized homonegativity (Grant, 2020b). It is within this conceptualization that the insidious and pervasive nature of hegemonic masculinity can be identified. Remember, hegemonic masculinity aids in sustaining patriarchal standards that position socialized masculinities over socialized femininities, and hierarchically ranks these masculinities based on their perceived approximation with femininity. Black same gender loving men often find themselves on the lower rungs of social masculine ranking due to their skin color, which is subordinated, and their sexual and romantic attractions, which are marginalized. This ranking creates an internalized hyperawareness of masculine appraisal, which then becomes externalized as some Black same gender loving men perceive risk in being in literal or perceived approximation to Black trans women. Hegemonic masculinity has influenced the subordinated and marginalized cisgender same gender loving Black man to incorrectly conflate sexual and romantic orientation with gender identity and project unjustifiable transphobia, by way of femmephobia, onto transgender women.

Transphobia is irrationality rooted within a system that seeks to maintain a gendered social order. From 2013 to 2020, violence against Black trans women has increased by at least 2.3 times (Human Rights Campaign, 2013; 2020). And although society often groups same gender loving folx and trans folx into one community, cognitive-behavioral conceptualizations suggest that the discomfort same gender loving men experience toward trans women triggers their sociopolitical distance from trans women and positions their complicity in the overall violences enacted upon trans women (Lavietes, 2019). Such complicit positioning parallels the historical navigation of white gay men who have been noted to receive the benefits of LGBTQ+ progression while ignoring the legal, healthcare, financial, and other disenfranchisements experienced by Black same gender loving folx (Nelson, Pantalone, & Carey, 2019; Nero, 2005; Stone & Ward, 2011; Ward, 2008).

What's your truth?

- Chapter one details the difference between sexual orientation and gender identity. Have you ever conflated the two, or seen them as the same? How have your perceptions of gender and sexual identity informed your thoughts around same gender loving identity? How have perceptions of gender and sexual identity informed your thoughts about trans identity?

We see it in sexual engagement

For those who may still be unmoved about the intersecting impact of hegemonic masculinity and femmephobia on Black livelihoods, I would like to turn readers' attention to the impact of these systems on sex. Men have been so conditioned to perceive approximation to femininity as a risk to their social privilege that they have even applied rigid masculine norms to the ways in which they approach themselves. While drafting this book, I polled various members of the Black community, through face-to-face and social media contact, on a simple question—"do you turn yourself on?" This is a complex question that, when scrutinized, has layered implications, yet I encouraged my audience to provide their automatic response. Out of a total sample size of almost 100 people ($n = 98$), most individuals ($n = 82$; 83%) provided an affirmative answer while others ($n = 16$, 17%) provided a negative response. Beyond the raw data, I was particularly intrigued by the demographic make-up of affirmative and negative responders, and those who chose not to respond. All of the individuals who stated that they turned themselves on identified as Black cisgender women, Black transgender women, and Black same gender loving men who felt affirmed in their sexual and romantic attraction (as evidenced by these individuals' social media presence and postings). I was immediately reminded of how those who often reject the rigid structures of hegemonic masculinity are oft afforded freedoms that transcend these structures.

All of the male respondents who denied turning themselves on ($n = 6$; 37%) identified as either heterosexual or same gender loving and conservative in their same gender loving identity expression (as evidenced by the hegemonically masculine presentations highlighted through their social media presence and postings). What stood further astounding was the recorded number of men who engaged with the survey yet chose not to provide an explicit response ($n = 60$). Of these men, 100% also identified as either Black and heterosexual, or Black, same gender loving, and conservative in their same gender loving identity expression (as evidenced by the hegemonically masculine presentations highlighted through their social media presence and postings). Although I chose not to follow up with these participants, I reflect on the number of men who did not engage in the survey and who provided a negative response. As this survey was disseminated to those in my immediate community, I am aware that many of these men engage in solo sex (i.e., masturbation), per their verbal report in spaces that call for the hegemonic portrayal of masculine performance (Grant, 2020b). There however seems to be a disconnect between these men's ability to engage in solo sex and their perception of being the object of their arousal. This phenomenon signifies a major impact of hegemonic masculinity on Black male sexual pleasure.

If these men who engage in solo sex are not being turned on by themselves, yet are using their bodies for sexual pleasure, have they allowed hegemonic masculinity to rob them of deeper emotional and sensual connectedness to self, due to fear of being self-perceived as same gender loving, or somehow aligned to the feminine? Hegemonic masculinity requires masculine dominance in addition to feminine separation. Hegemonic masculinity promotes the use of others for personal gain without emotional connection and concern for the object of pleasure's wellbeing (Connell & Messerschmidt, 2005; Hale & Ojeda, 2018). By this logic, a man who rejects the notion of being attracted to himself while engaging in solo sex has positioned himself in the sphere of hegemonic masculinity as both conqueror and conquered, colonizer and colonized, perpetrator and victim of objectification. He restricts himself from participating in the full immersion of solo sexual practice in order to reinforce that his idealized perception of masculinity has not been challenged.

Although a majority of same gender loving men in the presented poll noted being turned on by themselves, Black same gender loving men's sex lives are not left unaffected by the impact of hegemonic masculinity, heterosexism, and femmephobia. In 2019, I explored the phenomenon of bussy (i.e., anal) pain in Black same gender loving male sexual relationships in order to further understand the underlying mechanisms that have positioned this experience as a rite of passage among Black same gender loving men (Grant, 2020). The excavated literature supported that pain during anal penetration can be attributed to experiences of bussinismus—a psychophysiological anxiety or withdrawal Black male Bottoms experience before and/or during bussy penetration (Grant, 2019). Bussinismus occurs as a consequence of male Bottoms being socially perceived as submissive, fragile, and non-masculine (i.e., feminine). Due to their receptive sexual position, hegemonic masculinity and femmephobia have subordinated Black same gender loving Bottom masculinity and have aligned Bottoms with femininity. These influences have conditioned penetrative male partners to engage Bottoms through a lens of domination, similar to the manner in which heterosexual men engage heterosexual women—as property to be used for the satisfaction of the perceivably more dominant partner, and not as humans to be included in the partaking of mutual sexual satisfaction (Connell, 1995; Connell & Messerschmidt, 2005;

Grant, 2019; Hale & Ojeda, 2018). This dynamic emphasizes a dual process in which hegemonic masculinity and femmephobia are combined to affirm the subordinated and marginalized identities of the penetrating partner (i.e., the top) and further subordinate and marginalize the identities of the receptive partner (i.e., the Bottom). Such engagement creates a facade in which internalized homonegativity reinforces the concept of an idealized masculinity through the enaction of dominance in same gender loving sexual engagement.

What's your truth?

- Do you turn yourself on? Do you participate in solo sex? Why or why not?
- What are the influences that have informed your answer?

Truth: The triangular relationship between hegemonic masculinity, internalized homonegativity, and femmephobia is an extension of white supremacy

Many have highlighted that the perceived decrease in homophobia and expansion of acceptable masculinities reflect a reduction in the overall existence of hegemonic masculinity. It is true that masculine norms have changed over time—society has recently accepted and promoted men engaging in behaviors such as physical hygiene, emotional availability, mental health treatment, and intellectual expansion. Same sex attracted identities have gained increased visibility in mainstream culture; and legal, financial, and sociopolitical opportunities have been instituted to generally affirm the LGBTQ+ community. Nevertheless, to suggest that hegemonic masculinity, femmephobia, and internalized homonegativity are issues of the past is to create space for the blatant erasure of experiences that fall outside of a white context. While mainstream (i.e., white) culture is experiencing rapid structural changes that benefit gays, lesbians, bisexuals, and others in the spectrum of same sex sexual and romantic attraction, Black same gender loving folx often find themselves stunted in receiving these benefits, as the impacts of hegemonic masculinity, femmephobia, heterosexism, and internalized homonegativity still pervade the Black community. Black same gender loving men are still shaped by a conditioning which asserts that their masculinity, and accompanying privileges, can be measured and regulated. Hegemonic masculinity limits sexual pleasure for heterosexual and same gender loving Black men. Femmephobia keeps Black men hyperaware of their approximation to femininity, which continues to keep Black femmes (i.e., cisgender women, trans women, femme-identifying and performing men) at risk of multi-structural harm. These "isms" not only enforce a gender-based power hierarchy; they aid in positioning whiteness and white culture as more advanced, more progressive, and superior to non-white groups, cultures, and practices. A rage arises as one identifies the ways in which white supremacy has created heterosexist, homonegative, power structures that have ravaged non-white communities and have positioned these communities as inherently heterosexist and homonegative (Beam, 2008; Boykin & Shange, 2012; Griffin, 2010; hooks, 2004; Johnson, 2014; Snorton, 2014). And as the rippled effects of these structures still corrupt non-white communities, white supremacy has allowed for whiteness to perceivably transcend the negativity it has historically created.

4 Homonegativity and the Black Community

> "Doesn't the Sergeant know that there are men who from youth on desire women, and others, who are attracted only to men? Why then should he be punished now? After all, he knows not why God created him like this—that he can only love men!"
>
> –Same Sex Life Among a Few Negro Tribes of
> Angola, Part III (Falk,1923)

To understand the impact of homonegativity in the Black community is to acknowledge that homonegativity has severed the historical union between the Black community and same gender loving identity and practice. There exists a longstanding conviction among a certain sect within the African diaspora that same gender loving identity and practice as un-African, "against ... [African] nature," and/or a consequence of European, Arabic, and Asian colonization (McKaiser, 2012; Murray, Roscoe, & Epprecht, 2021; Tamale, 2014). This belief has fueled the anti-gay political stances, and homonegative legislative legacies, of world leaders such as Zimbabwe's Robert Mugabe, Nigeria's Goodluck Jonathan, and Uganda's Yoweri Museveni (Arimoro, 2018; McKay & Angotti, 2016; Muparamoto, 2020; Skock, 2021). This conviction has influenced the anti-gay rhetoric of Professor Griff from the hip-hop group Public Enemy, who in 1990 asserted that same gender lovingness did not exist in pre-colonial Africa, as there exists "no word in any African language" that describes a person who is gay, lesbian, bisexual, or any other term denoting non-heterosexuality (Murray, Roscoe, & Epprecht, 2021).[1] This stance has also influenced many African scholars to adamantly deny the historical presence of same gender lovingness on the Continent (Murray, Roscoe, & Epprecht, 2021). However, to support such a belief would be to blatantly ignore ethnographic identifications of same gender loving identity and practice

DOI: 10.4324/9781003180937-5

among Black folx, present prior to Africa's colonization and the enslavement of Africans.

Positioning same gender loving identity as un-African—not inherently Black—ignores the depiction of same gender sexual engagement found on rock paintings of the ancient the San people; it ignores the same gender loving practices of the sixteenth century royal and warrior inhabitants of modern-day Congo and Angola, who fought against first Portuguese colonizers of the Continent; it remains ignorant of the same gender loving practices among the royal and plebian people of the Dahomey kingdom in the eighteenth century; it ignores the Sudanic Mossi royals of the twentieth century, the highly esteemed same gender loving Dogon astrologers of Mali, the Bambara, the Dagara of Burkina Fasso, and the same gender loving practices of community heads, spiritual leaders, and other persons from Togo, Ghana, Ivory Coast, Liberia, Nigeria, Senegal, and South, Southeast, and Southwest Africa (whose practices and identities have been ethnographically recorded as recently as the 1990s) (Murray, Roscoe, & Epprecht, 2021). To deny same gender loving identity's connection to Blackness, or African identity, also erases the present presence of well adjusted, well-rounded, thriving same gender loving folx and organizations in Nigeria, Ghana, Zimbabwe, Uganda, southern Africa, and other areas of the Continent (Murray, Roscoe, & Epprecht, 2021).

Regarding language, Stephan O. Murray's (2021) *Boy-wives and Female Husbands* confirms the lack of explicit historical vocabulary that corresponds with Western labels such as gay, lesbian, bisexual, and queer. However, the investigations of Murray (2021) and his contemporaries emphasize that decolonized understanding of traditional African sexualities cannot be achieved by using colonial tools. The absence of same gender loving African labels that correspond with a Eurocentric lens of understanding does not denote the absence of same gender loving identity, practice, and relationship from African culture. The ethnographic findings amassed from Niger-Congo, Bantu, Afro-Asiatic, Khoisan, and Nilo-Saharan communities highlight an extensive lexicon that brings awareness to, and representation of, vocabulary denoting same gender loving diviners and prophets (*kimbanda, mwaami*), anal intercourse (*jiegele ketön, okutunduka vanena*), mutual masturbation between the same genders (*ôa-/huru, /huru*), same gender erotic friendship (*oupanga*), boy-wives (*ndon-go-techi-la, nkhonsthana, tinkonkana, nkonkana*) same gender loving male lovers (*eponji*), and homosexuality (*gaglgo*) (Murray, Roscoe, & Epprecht, 2021).

Asserting that no African language exists to capture same gender experiences propagates seeds of ignorance and confusion. Same gender loving relationships have a historical presence on the African continent and were expressed in ways that transcend modern conceptualizations of same gender loving life. Murray, Roscoe, & Epprecht (2021) highlight how same gender loving relationships were often engaged based on age (e.g., older individuals paying a bride price to engage in relationships with younger members of the community), gender expression (e.g., men who displayed feminine affect or aesthetic features being courted, romanced, and pursued by men who adhered to masculine norms), and egalitarian segregation (e.g., numerous accounts of same gender sexual and romantic engagement between age- and status-equal peers throughout the lifespan are recorded in various communities, and frequently represented in spaces in which cisgender men and women are separated by gender) (Falk, 1923; Somé, 1993; Weeks 1909). The writers also note that in some cultures, heterosexual marriage and reproduction were often perceived as duties to be fulfilled by all biologically able members of a community; however, same gender sexual and romantic satisfaction were often accepted once the heterosexual duties were fulfilled. What stands more fascinating is that many members of these traditional communities possessed no rigid conceptualization or adherence to labels such as gay, lesbian, etc. Such norms depict a fluidity in the traditional presentations of sexuality and highlight how Western understandings of same gender loving identity inadequately conceptualize African sexualities. This is most notably evidenced by the ways European ethnographers saturated their observational records of traditional African culture with projections of white supremacist morals, values, and prejudices against African people (Murray, Roscoe, & Epprecht, 2021).

Truth exploration: Are Black folx more homonegative than other races?

> There was a joke someone told once and it was like, "Don't you know? Black people can't be gay!"
>
> Simeon, 31, Brooklyn, NY

Following discourse of the natural presence of same gender loving identity and practice throughout the African diaspora is an equally divisive consideration of whether Black folx are more homonegative in comparison to their white counterparts and other racial groups. Research, qualitative narrative, and documented accounts position homonegativity as embedded in Black culture (Beam, 2008; Grant, 2020, 2010; Johnson, 2014). This presentation has become so pervasive that many scholars, clinicians, and observers of Black life may perceive homonegativity in the Black community, family, church, and other spaces as common to the Black experience. However, in order to honor the nuanced African histories, religions, communities, and cultural practices that have been stripped and distorted by white colonialism and white supremacy, I must challenge the notion that Black folx are inherently homonegative. Same gender loving identity and practice became stigmatized, disenfranchised, and marginalized when "native Africans became indoctrinated into colonial practice and began to forget the historical presence of same gender loving patterns within the culture" (Murray, Roscoe, & Epprecht, 2021). The indoctrination of enslaved Africans into Eurocentric culture erased the pan-Africanist acceptance, preservation, and expression of diverse sexuality, and further laid the foundations for the institutionalization of homonegativity in the Black community. It will never be the purpose of this work to suggest that Black folx are more homonegative than the rest of the human population. What stands apparent, however, is that Black folx have been embedded in a social system that has distorted their representations of diverse sexualities, which has propagated generational homonegativity.

What's your truth?

- What are your thoughts, perceptions, and experiences regarding the Black community and homonegativity?
- How do you believe homonegativity in the Black community compares to other races?
- Why do you think Black folx are positioned as more homonegative than other racial groups?

Truth: Homonegativity in the Black community is linked to Black survival in a white supremacist world

Despite the rich ethnographic literature that highlights how unenslaved African men navigated same sex attraction sans homonegativity, present writings suggest that internalized homonegativity among Black men may have origins in pre-colonial conceptualizations of Black sexuality and post-colonial enslavement (hooks, 2004; Lemelle, 2010; Murray, Roscoe, & Epprecht, 2021). Before the appearance of the Portuguese in Africa, there existed the myth of the "primitive man" (some would argue that such a myth has sustained itself in present culture to justify the disenfranchisement and murder of Black people in 2021) (Collins, 2004; Murray, Roscoe, & Epprecht, 2021). Africans were perceived by

Europeans as untamed, inferior, savage beings—with deviant sexualities often compared to animals—solely purposed for reproduction (Collins, 2004; hooks, 2004; Murray, Roscoe, & Epprecht, 2021; Nederveen Pieterse, 1992). This portrayal of Black livelihood and Black sexuality intensified and expanded as European ethnographers became peripherally privy to the diverse and complex presentations of sex, sexuality, and gender expression found among native African people. Murray, Roscoe, & Epprecht (2021) aptly remind readers that "the colonialists did not introduce homosexuality to Africa but rather the intolerance of it—and the systems of surveillance and regulation for suppressing it" (Murray, Roscoe, & Epprecht, 2021). These systems of surveillance and regulation can be identified within African nations since colonization and have been present in the experiences of Black folx since enslavement (Arimoro, 2018; McKay & Angotti, 2016; Muparamoto, 2020; Skock, 2021).

History presents the ways in which Black people have been perceived as expendable property to be dehumanized, manipulated, and used for the accumulation and maintenance of white wealth (hooks, 2004; Snorton, 2014). Europeans used labels of baseness, savagery, primitivity, and deviance to exploit and enslave native Africans (Nederveen Pieterse, 1992). These exploitations are noted through the historical media characterizations of Black women as Jezebels and Mammies, or Black men as Bucks or Sambos (Bowleg et al., 2013; Collins, 2004; hooks, 2004; Nederveen Pieterse, 1992; Stayhorn, 2008; Strayhorn & Tillman-Kelly, 2013). Nederveen Pieterse's (1992) investigation of Black trope formation in Western culture highlights Eurocentric efforts to explain Black people and Black cultural practices, and to justify the maleficence enacted on Blacks by whites throughout history. The Black Buck is a historical trope that presents Black men as sexually insatiable brutes, whose sole intention is to rob white women of their sexual purity (Nederveen Pieterse, 1992). Neverdeen Pierterse (1992) describes the Sambo as a Eurocentric trope that presents Black men as a lazy, knock-kneed, jester-like individuals who enjoy life under white dominance. The Jezebel, like the Buck, has been used to present Black women as lustful and nymphomaniacal; whereas the Mammie trope, having evolved throughout history, has depicted a warm-natured, usually asexual, Black woman who enjoys caring for white adults and children, even at the cost of neglecting her own offspring (Nederveen Pieterse, 1992). While the characterization of the Black Buck and Jezebel were used to justify the lynching and raping of Black men and women, the representations of the Mammie and Sambo were dispersed to perpetuate the idea that some Black folx were void of sexuality and created for the sole purpose of serving whites (Nederveen Pieterse, 1992). These early characterizations placed Black folx on an oppressive binary of hypersexual or sexually void, which further normalized and justified their sexual exploitation (Nederveen Pieterse, 1992).

The historical exploitation, regulation, and suppression of Black sexuality can also be observed in the relationship between the enslaved African and overseer. Snorton's (2014)*Nobody Has to Know* describes how the physical and sexual violence enacted by overseers and masters planted seeds of helplessness among enslaved male and female Africans (Collins, 2004). Such traumas influenced enslaved Africans to resist white control through the construction of customs hidden from the white gaze. Snorton (2014) notes that despite oppression, enslaved African in the United States explored their sexualities and romances in secret and curated their own "closet"s which begat traditions such as "jumping the broom" (a practice in which an enslaved African couple, whose marriage was legally and systemically unrecognized, jumped over a broom to publicly acknowledge their marital union) (Nederveen Pieterse, 1992; Snorton, 2014). This example emphasizes the way Black folx have had to historically hide their sexualities, and serves as a foundation for understanding sexual secrecy and homonegativity in the Black community (Lemelle, 2010; Snorton 2014). Observing the resilient preservation of Black sexual and romantic practices during and after enslavement further highlights how whiteness—despite its distortive impact on Black identity—has been historically unable and ill-equipped to grasp and honor the complexities of Black sexuality.

In *We Real Cool: Black Men and Masculinity*, bell hooks (2004) provides increased insight into the evolution of Black sexual repression. hooks (2004) informs readers that the sexual exploitation of enslaved Africans was only the initial influence on the culture of Black sexual restriction and regulation in America. She notes that the abolition of slavery ushered in Reconstruction, the Great Migration, and national economic difficulties. hooks (2004) further highlights that this era was tapestried with heightened anxieties toward Black sexuality, as evidenced by works such as *the Birth of a* Nation, the emergence of the Klu Klux Klan, and the increased criminalization of drug distribution and use, prostitution, and other identified "deviant behaviors" (Collins, 2004; hooks, 2004; Snorton, 2014). This social climate begat a communal striving, particularly among the Black bourgeoisie, to reinstate and reaffirm Black humanity, and position the Black community as both socially accepted by, and morally superior to, the white majority (Snorton, 2014; Stone, 2011; Stoler, 1989). E. Franklin

Frazier notes that Black folx at this time, "strove to mold themselves in the image of the white man," as many African Americans perceived social and moral elevation as solely achievable through the replication of Eurocentric middle-class social values, appetites, and standards (hooks, 2004; Snorton 2014; Schwarz, 2003).

While the Black community seemed freed from the sexual policing perpetuated during slavery (although literature speaks of the race-based sexual stereotyping, anxieties, and life-threatening policing Black people endured post-slavery), intracommunal Black sexual repression, mainly perpetuated by the working-class and privileged Blacks, became increasingly viewed as a means of obtaining communal elevation (Lemelle, 2010; Snorton, 2014; Stone, 2011; Summer, 2004). Literature highlights how respectability and a budding "race survival consciousness" in the Black community demanded the performance of rigid scripts, which included adherence to gender roles and hegemonic masculinity as a means of Black preservation and progression (Crichlow, 2004; hooks, 2004; Collins, 2004; Lemelle & Battle, 2004; Schwarz, 2003; Snorton, 2014). It is interesting to note that the white ideals which structured these scripts could never be fully achieved, as sociocultural structures that shaped American society—which include the oversaturation of Black women over Black men in the labor work workforce—interrupted the gendered expectations of the working male husband and female housewife (Schwarz, 2003). However, from the norms of respectability and adherence to traditional gender scripts stemmed the development of unique Black masculine tropes, such as the "sweetback"—a characterization of Black masculinity which rested on shrouding social incapacity (i.e., financial and employment insecurity) and asserting masculine dominance through the financial and sexual manipulation of multiple women (Schwarz, 2003). Norms of respectability further called for the highlighting, marginalization, and degradation of same gender loving identity (hooks, 2004; Schwarz, 2003; Snorton, 2014). The early 1900s introduced the idea that same gender loving identity and practice originated among European whites (Schwarz, 2003). Accompanied were the beliefs that same gender loving proclivities could be transmitted like communicable diseases, and that same gender loving people were predators focused on spreading the disease of same gender loving identity (Schwarz, 2003). These messages were systemically perpetuated in the Black community (by the Black bourgeoisie and working class through print media and social politics) in order to justify xenophobic distancing from same gender loving identity, promote a regulation and suppression of same gender loving activity, and influence adherence to norms of respectability (Schwarz, 2003).

Even through moments of Black liberation, such as the Harlem Renaissance and the Civil Rights era—when many Black people resisted respectability politics and engaged in noted sexual revolutions—hegemonic gendered scripts were adhered to by Black men and women (hooks, 2004; Stone, 2011; Summers, 2004; Whiting & Lewis, 2008). The rise of hegemonic norms in the Black community throughout the 1900s produced an intolerance for any presentations that transcended rigidly gendered, male-female binary, scripts. The 1965 Moynihan Report exemplifies efforts to promote adherence to Black hegemony, as it emphasized that sexual performance outside of heteronormativity hindered Black progression and degraded the Black family (hooks, 2004; Snorton, 2014). Such messaging, that has shaped the Black community, provides context for Black folk who have engaged in the homonegative avoidance of understanding, investigating, expressing, or accepting diverse sexualities (Battle & Bennett, 2008; hooks, 2004; Snorton, 2014; Summers, 2004). Such messaging has also influenced some in the Black community to internalize homonegative associations, such as that between Black same gender loving identity and HIV/AIDS (Moseby, 2017). Intracommunal homonegativity has served as a conduit to internalized homonegativity, which has left many Black same gender loving men in a state of suffering and malfunctioning in various domains (hooks 2014; Lemelle, 2010; Loiacano, 1989; McCune, 2008; Snorton, 2014; Shoptaw, et al., 2009; Winder, 2015). Research suggests that in order to be accepted by their racial community, Black men are expected to identify with and perform heterosexuality, dominance and aggression toward women, and emotional unavailability (hooks 2014; Lemelle, 2010; Loiacano, 1989; McCune, 2008). Literature supports how Black men who go against their expected societal performance risk being labeled same gender loving and ostracized by their racial community (Grant, 2020; Lemelle, 2010; Loiacano, 1989; Snorton, 2014; Winder, 2015). Such is the way in which white supremacist ideologies have pervaded and distorted traditional African culture and account for the current regulation and suppression of Black same gender loving male identity.

Note

1 Public Enemy leader Chuck D has since supported Barack Obama's legislative support of the LGBT community and has spoken against homonegativity in hip hop culture (Garcia, 2012).

5 Homonegativity and the Black Church

I will always view the Black church—that is, the Black Christian religious institution—as a beautiful and imperfect space that both enriches and challenges one's life. The Black church's customs have often nurtured and fortified the spirit, while its members have often expressed a hyperawareness of same gender loving affect, and have used that hyperawareness to prey upon those perceived to be same gender loving. In 2004, I recall attending a church camping trip that united members of my Christian denomination from all over the world. This trip was a soul-stirring experience that exposed me to the transcendental nature of spiritual practice. This trip was also shaped, however, by other distinct memories, which include morning worship services saturated with homonegative rhetoric. In 2016, the spiritual fervor I felt in my youth transformed as I developed into adulthood. During my tenure as leader of my church's music department, members of my church used my presence on social media to "out" my sexual orientation to the congregation. This effort consequentially led to my resignation from church leadership and my temporary adoption of religious apathy. My experiences and explorations with other Black same gender loving men have highlighted that the Black church is a multifaceted and complex institution; the Black church's impact on Black same gender loving men's development reveals a historical relationship that highlights themes of liberation, oppression, freedom, and bondage.

Truth: The Black church has often positioned itself as a beacon of hope and homonegativity

The Black church stands as a pillar in the Black community that has played an instrumental role in the Black family and communal life throughout history (Foster, Arnold, Rebchook, & Kegels, 2011; Jeffries,

DOI: 10.4324/9781003180937-6

Dodge, & Sandfort, 2008; Ward, 2005; Winder, 2015). Record recounts the Black church's position as a support, change instrument, and liberating space for Black people before and after emancipation, during the Civil Rights era, and presently. Unfortunately, the Black church has also been identified as a space where homophobic rhetoric is disseminated and homonegativity is perpetuated throughout the Black community (Foster, Arnold, Rebchook, and Kegels, 2011; Garrett-Walker & Torres, 2016; Jeffries, Dodge, & Sandfort, 2008; Ward, 2005; Winder, 2015). By serving as the authority that dictates and differentiates the holy from the abominable, the Black church has been positioned to have institutional control over Black sexuality—paralleling the dynamic of white colonizers over enslaved Africans—and to act as a communal power that determines acceptable and intolerable expressions of Black masculinity (hooks, 2004; Jeffries, Dodge, & Sandfort, 2008; Ward, 2005). History notes how notorious leaders of the Black church, such as Rev. Adam Clayton Powell of Harlem's Abyssinian Baptist Church, was the first to "initiate a vigorous crusade against homosexuality," which emboldened other clergymen to follow in his example (Griffin, 2010). Studies present that some Black churches serve as hostile and intolerant institutional spheres in which Black same gender loving men may be barred from leadership positions; may be invited to assume leadership positions in exchange for concealing their same gender loving status; or may become the subject of homonegative sermons or congregational rumors (Griffin, 2010; Snorton, 2014; Tennial, 2015; Ward, 2005; Winder, 2015). At the intersection of community dominance and sexual repression and regulation exists the Black church's contribution to homonegativity within the Black community (Garrett-Walker & Torres, 2016; Ward, 2005).

The Black church is recognized as an assembly of churches that are predominantly Protestant and predominantly led and attended by Black individuals (Griffin, 2010). The Black church is also noted to possess clear cultural and traditional differences from predominantly white Judeo-Christian institutions (Griffin, 2010). The Black church is largely understood to be comprised of the National Baptist Convention, the National Baptist Convention of America, the Progressive National Convention, the African Methodist Episcopal Church, the African Methodist Episcopal Zion Church, the Christian Methodist Episcopal Church, and the Church of God in Christ (Butler & Walton, 2021). Despite their unique narratives of development, all denominations within the Black church have taken a generally oppositive stance against same gender loving identity, practice, and affirmation. It is not uncommon to witness church leaders cite biblical texts (Genesis 1&2, 19:1–9; Leviticus

18:22, 20:13; 1 Corinthians 6:9; Romans 1:26–27; and 1 Timothy 1:10) to justify their homonegative stances. Despite the institutional efforts to restrict same gender loving presence in the Black church, same gender loving men and women have continued to thrive and assume space in all facets of religious life; and have been documented to receive substantial lifespan benefits from being involved in religious spaces (Winder, 2015). Research highlights how in addition to spiritual upliftment and the chance to expand and develop skills in music, theater, and oration, the church often offers same gender loving people the opportunity to engage in cohort bonding and sexual and romantic partner pairing with other same gender loving folx (Pitt, 2010; Walker & Longmire-Avital, 2013; Winder, 2015). Ethnographic literature further suggests that these benefits can lead Black same gender loving men to experience higher qualities of life despite the marginalization they may experience in nonreligious spaces (hooks, 2004; Snorton, 2014). However, the Black church's homonegative stances restrict same gender loving people from full integration into the Black religious experience; and same gender loving folx's resilience and assumed benefits from religious engagement cannot overshadow the risks (mental, physical, sexual, etc.) that arise when same gender loving folx chronically exist in spaces that are intolerant and non-affirming of their full identities (Barnes & Meyer, 2012; Dangerfield et al., 2019; Heard Harvey & Ricard, 2018; Moore, Robinson, Dailey, & Thompson, 2015). The desire to be accepted by a homonegative religious community often places same gender loving men at odds with themselves and keeps them engaged in a conflict that is sometimes left unresolved (Griffin, 2010; Tennial, 2015).

> To be honest, I have no positive experiences from being raised in the Black church. It was extremely difficult having to constantly hear how homosexuality is a sin. If we're discussing money troubles or if the sermon is about something on another subject, why does it have to revert to sexuality being the reason people have money troubles? Things like that. It would be difficult having to constantly hear, "Stop the homosexuality. Stop loving men." It's like, what does that have to do with someone having a foreclosure on their house? It was constantly hearing that every Sunday that separated me from the Black church.
>
> Devin, 30, Charleston, SC

> How can something say, "God loves you in spite of" and "God knows your life before you enter this earth," and yet "God hates gay people?" I get confused with that. If He does and He knew

what my life was going to be, how did I get presented this opportunity to be on this earth if He wasn't a fan of it?

Edgar, 30, Lawnside, NJ

I weed out the negativity that comes from heterosexual folx in church because as I think about my relationship with God. I know that God loves everyone, and he created everyone equally and he created me to be who I am today. I was born a same gender loving man; it's not something that was taught to me. And I firmly believe that because He made me this way, He loves me. And I'm going to continue having my relationship with Him, regardless of what anyone in the church says.

Chris, 30, Charlotte, NC

For your consideration: A tale of two singers

Same gender loving people have always existed in the religious sphere. In fact, many same gender loving people have been integral to the formation and preservation of the Black religious institution (Griffin, 2010; Tennial, 2015). Same gender loving men have been noted to historically serve as spiritual gate keepers and religious leaders throughout pre-colonized Africa (Murray, Roscoe, & Epprecht, 2021). Folx like Reverend Yvette Flunder, members of the Hawkins Singers, and Reverend James Cleveland have been notorious for their influence on gospel music and their positions as same gender loving individuals (Dade, 2012). Even more recently, B.Slade (formerly known as Tonex) and Darrell Walls of the Walls Groups have served as more contemporary reminders that the Black church and its statutes have never been successful in suppressing same gender loving people or separating same gender loving people from their ministerial impact (Dade, 2012; Hudson, 2020). There nevertheless remains some Black same gender loving folx who have been harmed by their indoctrination in the Black church's homonegative beliefs.

Singer and regarded gospel legend, Daryl Coley, transitioned from this world in 2016 having left as part of his legacy a wife and advertised struggle with homosexuality (Tennial, 2014). For decades, the Black church has watched silently as gospel singer Donnie McClurkin has struggled to accept his same gender loving desires; and has used communal support to complicitly rewarded McClurkin for his denial of self (Tennial, 2014). McClurkin has blamed his same gender loving desires on experienced childhood molestation, which perpetuates false narratives that same gender loving people are predators, and that same gender loving identity is a condition that can be transmitted (Schwartz, 2003; Tennial, 2014). McClurkin, one who once betrothed himself to women, has also now resigned himself to a life of singledom as he notes he "doesn't know how to be with a woman" (Barnes & Meyer, 2012; The Source, 2021). It is not the purpose of this text to evaluate McClurkin's journey. It is, however, the work of this text to normalize McClurkin's experience as one had by many same gender loving men involved in the Black church—preachers, elders, deacons, music ministers, ushers, congregants (Tennial, 2015). It is also the work of this text to inquire how long the Black church will be complicit—through silence and reinforcement with communal praise—in allowing these harmful patterns to continue. When will the biblical texts that allegedly justify homonegative stances be replaced by reminders that Black same gender loving men are "fearfully and wonderfully made" and destined for a "purpose [that secures]... hope and a future?" Until a change occurs in rhetoric and action, many Black same gender loving men will continue to suffer within an institution they seek to serve.

> This is where the mannerisms come into play because being someone who was a lead singer at the church, back then I was thinking, "Okay, how can I make it seem like it was my brother singing and not me? How can I make the people in the audience not see me?" Because if they see me, they won't understand what I'm singing. It'll be like them expecting Jesus and Beyoncé shows up. It's someone totally different giving you a message. I think that's the difficulty I had navigating the Black church. It contributed to me not singing as I got older because I didn't know how to perform.
>
> Rammy, 30, Wilson, NC

Truth: The Black church must give an account for the way it has contributed to the stigma surrounding HIV/AIDS and the loss of Black same gender lives during the HIV/AIDS crisis

In 2018, Black/African American folx represented 13% of the United States population yet accounted for 42% (16,002) of 37,968 new HIV diagnoses in the United States (Centers for Disease Control & Prevention, 2021). Of the 42% of new cases in the Black community, Black same gender loving men represented 59% (9,444) in 2018. This overrepresentation only reflects the historic burden of HIV/AIDS multiple generations of Black same gender loving men have carried, often without support from the Black church (Griffin, 2010). The Black church's homonegative teachings, and inaction around same gender loving male sexual health promotion and risk reduction, have been noted to significantly add to HIV/AIDS contraction, proliferation, and mortality-related disparities within this demographic (Griffin, 2010). The homonegative teachings of the church have also aided in strengthening the fallible association between Black same gender loving male identity and disease susceptibility, and have positioned HIV/AIDS as a retributive consequence for same gender loving identity and sexual and romantic behavior (Griffin, 2010; Garrett-Walker & Torres, 2016; Jeffries, Dodge, & Sandfort, 2008; Winder, 2015). In an attempt to balance the presentation of this history, it should be noted that there exist Black religious institutions that have fully engaged in combating HIV/AIDS stigma, in promoting HIV/AIDS awareness with anti-homonegative approaches, in providing HIV/AIDS education, and in using compassionate and culturally humble methods to treat those impacted by HIV/AIDS (Ward, 2005). However, record highlights the tendencies of these organizations to minimize the relevance of same gender loving identity—to engage in same gender loving identity erasure by emphasizing care provided to the general population—as a component of reducing stigma and providing intervention (Ward, 2005). Although same gender loving folx are not solely affected by HIV/AIDS, such erasure emphasizes the challenges that must still be overcome when pursuing the full integration and affirmation of same gender loving people in the Black church.

Truth: Religious relationship does not reflect spiritual relationship

Although research focuses on Black same gender loving men's relationship with religion/religiosity and the Black church, little literature investigates Black same gender loving men's relationship with spirituality and religious exploration beyond same gender loving oppression. Miller (2007) attempted to contribute to this dearth by investigating the spiritual experiences of HIV-positive Black same gender loving men. His qualitative results highlighted Black same gender loving men who once possessed close ties to the church, yet developed a stance in which they refused to allow their love for the Black church to force them to endure the hate disseminated from leaders and congregants of the institution. These men noted how their religious journeys, greatly shaped by social engagement and connection, influenced their refusal to exist in spaces that did not affirm all their identities (Miller, 2007; Pitt, 2009).

Many of the participants in my dissertation had similar experiences, in which they distanced themselves from the church and refused to engage in religious spaces that were non-affirming. Some participants changed their denominations, while others forsook their engagement in church and adopted an identity centered on an individual nurturing of spirit (Grant, 2020b). These participants viewed spirituality as a personal relationship with their higher being and engaged in activities such as meditation and prayer. Other participants sought studies in other religions and doctrines, which include Islam and Buddhism. It is interesting to note, however, that some of the Black same gender loving men I have interviewed were often wary of sharing their exploration of spirituality and religion with other members of the Black church. One participant in my dissertation noted:

> I think the fact that if I say that I am not Christian, how it makes then other people feel uncomfortable with their Christian beliefs. Can they then engage with me? Am I seen as human? Am I seen as even more deviant than I already quote-unquote can be? I think it's like the idea of still trying to present as straight. There's still then this proximity to privilege that I want to be able to have because if I don't identify as Christian, then that continues to further subjugate me to the margins.
>
> (Grant, 2020b)

This participant not only recognizes the Black church as an institution for spiritual growth but identifies being a Black Christian as a marker of social capital in the Black community. To profess affiliation with a non-Christian religion, while also same gender loving, would be to further marginalize himself in the eyes of those who exist in this institution. Such an acknowledgment provides possible insight into the factors—privilege, social capitol, and the desire for community—that motivate many Black same gender loving men to stay within the institution of the Black church, despite the homonegative experiences that pervade the space.

> It's what we know. If you're groomed to be a dancer at a young age, despite the things that come with it, you're going to do it. I'm thinking about myself; why I was in the church for so long was because it was all I knew. My family was involved in it and I was good at something there. If I didn't sing, I really don't know if I

would have stayed in the church that long. And a lot of same gender loving people—we play, we sing, we preach, we direct choirs, we have groups. It's our outlet.

Avery, 33, Washington, D.C.

Reframing: Are we giving the Black church too much credit for homonegativity?

There is ease in colluding with the idea that the Black church, at its core, is one of the main sources of homonegativity in the Black community. Research provides numerous examples of the homonegativity and same gender loving marginalization that occurs in the church (Foster, Arnold, Rebchook, & Kegels, 2011; Garrett-Walker & Torres, 2016; Jeffries, Dodge, & Sandfort, 2008; Tennial, 2015; Ward, 2005; Winder, 2015). There however exists budding literature that suggests fallibility in the zeitgeist that popularly positions the Black church as a regulator of homonegativity in the Black community (Irizarry & Perry, 2017). There has appeared an increase of churches in the Black community that preach same gender loving acceptance, affirmation, healing, and inclusion (Pitt, 2010; White et al., 2019). Some heterosexual religious leaders and gospel influencers have also stepped forth to condemn the homonegativity that exists in the Black church (Witherspoon, 2015). These occurrences prompt observers to reevaluate whether the Black church can assume responsibility for broader homonegativity in the Black community.

Irizarry and Perry (2017) provide considerations against the narrative of the Black church's power and homonegative influence on the Black community, and prompt readers to further examine the complexities surrounding the relationship between the Black church and the Black community. Irizarry and Perry (2017) examine messages disseminated from the Black church and remind readers that the presence of homonegative rhetoric from the church, or church leaders, does not signify congregational agreement with homonegativity (i.e., the presence of rhetoric does not equate to the Black community's reception or adoption of homonegativity). Their research, which compared Black and white, 2004–2014, General Social Survey attitudes toward same gender loving identity, same sex civil rights (i.e., the right to marry), same sex sexual practice (i.e., the right to engage in sex), and the impact of religiosity on these views, suggests that religion and religiosity provide limited bases for homonegative attitudes. Instead, results of the study highlight the impact of socioeconomic status and education—markers of social privilege—on homonegative views (Grant, 2020b; Lefevor et al., 2020; Irizarry & Perry, 2017; Schulte & Battle, 2004). The study presents that Black folx with 4-year college degrees and graduate degrees endorsed more homonegative views than Black people who possessed a high school education or lower. Further, Black folx who earned salaries in the second to fourth quintiles (i.e., middle class) endorsed more homonegative attitudes than those who fell in the top and bottom earning categories (Lefevor et al., 2020; Irizarry & Perry, 2017).

Chapter four noted the way in which respectability politics in the Black community—which stemmed from an effort to no longer be perceived as "highly sexualized devious beings by the white gaze"—was most championed by those considered at the time to be the Black bourgeoise—a cohort that, due to the era's social system, was comprised of both working-class and upper-class individuals (Griffin, 2010; Schwartz, 2003). It was this working elite who held enough social and financial capital to disseminate homonegative messages in printed media, in coveted social groups, and in religious spaces. As education has become more widely accessible, and socioeconomic divides more widely noticeable, there arises observation that the traditional values found among the Black bourgeoise are values that have helped secure the maintenance of the Black middle class. E. Franklin Frazier described the Black church as "an institution within an institution," which emphasizes that the values and messages touted from the church reflect the values of those who hold power, resource, and representation within the institution (Griffin, 2010). The homonegative values and rhetoric disseminated throughout the Black church may therefore be less a presentation of moral conviction, and more of perpetuation of Black middle-class expectations of respectability that have been historically preached, rewarded, and reinforced in the Black community by the Black middle-class.

Clinician's corner on praying the gay away

Many Black same gender loving men who live with internalized homonegativity sometimes engage in a practice of "praying the gay away"—they believe that they can erase their same gender loving identity through prayer, penitence, and religious involvement. This praxis reflects a greater belief that positions same gender loving identity as wrong. How do your beliefs align or contrast with this position? If a client came to you and disclosed his participation in this behavior, what would be your therapeutic inclinations? Robertson & Avent (2016) emphasize the importance of understanding personal beliefs and professional responsibilities when treating same gender loving folx. Therapeutic responsibility includes making the treatment space safe by understanding and normalizing clients' experiences and further understanding their goals for treatment. What are some concerns you have about affirming the experiences of same gender loving clients who may endorse strong homonegative ideals?

6 Homonegativity and Black Families

Many of the homonegative messages perpetuated throughout the Black community are often centered around Black same gender loving men's alleged negative impact on the Black family. Black same gender loving men have been historically labeled a predatorial danger to Black youth (Schwarz, 2003). Black same gender loving men are often characterized as sexually deviant and erroneously connected with generalizations, such as being the cause of HIV proliferation in the Black community due to their propensity to engage in promiscuous behavior with heterosexual and same gender loving individuals (Boykin, 2006; Snorton, 2014). Black same gender loving men's perceived inability to fit the mold of idealized Black masculinity has positioned them as scapegoats for the deterioration of Black manhood and the Black family (Griffin, 2010). Such characterizations are often used to maintain hyperawareness of Black same gender loving male identity, provide fallacy ridden justifications for the communal mistreatment of Black same gender loving men, and keep many members of the Black community blind to the detrimental effects some familial patterns have on Black same gender loving male functioning and development. Research has identified perceived familial rejection, actual familial rejection, and experienced familial abuse due to sexual orientation as factors that have deleterious impacts on Black same gender loving men's sexual development, sexual health outcomes, and experiences of internalized homonegativity (D'Augelli, Grossman, & Starks, 2005; Jadwin-Cakmak, Pingel, Harper, & Bauermeister, 2015; Lasala & Frierson, 2012; Savin-Williams, 1994). And although research often positions the Black family as inherently homonegative, deeper excavation into the experiences of Black same gender loving men may provide nuanced insight into the factors that influence homonegativity among Black families.

DOI: 10.4324/9781003180937-7

Truth: Homonegativity in Black families may be related to more than same gender sexual and romantic attraction

Literature suggests that homonegativity among Black same gender loving men originates in the interactions between Black same gender loving youth and their parental figure(s); and suggests that the homonegativity exhibited by parents of Black same gender loving male youth may reflect parental anxieties that arise when parents perceive their son as unable to fit behavioral expectations of Black masculinity (LaSala & Frierson, 2012; Rosario, Rotheram-Borus, & Reid, 1996). In 2005, D'Augelli, Grossman, and Starks (2005) conducted a study that examined the parental awareness of gay identity among 293 youth. Although Black same gender loving youth made up a minority of the sample (*n* = 69; 23.5%), results communicated that parents' first inclination toward their child's same gender loving status did not stem from witnessing their child participate in same gender loving sexual or romantic engagement. Instead, the first awareness of the child's same gender loving identity was postulated from the child's "gender-atypical performance"—meaning, the child's display of behavior that was incongruent with the gender role expectations constructed by the family and greater social community (D'Augelli, Grossman, & Starks, 2005; Horn & Wong, 2014). In the case of Black same gender loving male youth, atypical or non-masculine gender performance often prompts family members to assume that their male child may have same gender sexual or romantic attractions.

Qualitative data, from parents of same gender loving Black boys, communicate caregivers' first awareness of a parent–child relationship strain that arose when they perceived their sons to exhibit gender-atypical behaviors, regardless of whether their sons had "come out" (Fields, Bogart, Smith, & Malebranche, 2015; Lasala & Frierson, 2012). Research posits that such recognition highlights caregiver fears that, due to their son's same gender loving orientation (via behavioral expression), the Black same gender loving youth will be unable to fulfill expectations of Black masculinity, which include behaviors such as engaging in heterosexual unions and producing biological offspring (Lasala & Frierson, 2012; Rosario, Rotheram-Borus, & Reid, 1996). Such behaviors are not inherently masculine, as masculinity changes with cultural context. These behaviors, however, are rooted in both community sustaining expectations that have origins in precolonized Africa, as well as more oppressive requirements placed upon enslaved male Africans, who were sexually exploited to produce more enslaved offspring (Murray, Roscoe, &

Epprecht, 2021). The perspectives of the surveyed parents highlight a culmination of inherited gender role performance values and communal expectations, that become perceivably disrupted when a Black male identifies as same gender loving, or expresses affect assumed to align with same gender loving identity.

Fields, Bogart, Smith, and Malebranche (2015) further explain this phenomenon by presenting how gender role strain can impact the relationship between Black same gender loving youth and their families. Gender role strain is an umbrella term that encompasses the "psychological distress associated with failing to meet masculine ideals [known as *discrepancy strain*], difficulty enacting and maintaining normative masculine expression [regarded as *dysfunction strain*], and negative experience with the masculine socialization process [classified as *trauma strain*]." Black same gender loving male youth often experience trauma strain through their difficulty to adhere to the homonegative and hypermasculine expectations of their families and communities, which include "challenging authority... heterosexual hypersexuality... [emotional overcontrol and] toughness...being physically strong and aggressive... [and] avoiding effeminate behavior" (Fields, Bogart, Smith, & Malebranche, 2015; Flannigan-Saint-Aubin, 1993). The parents and guardians of these youth may often be attuned to their son's juxtaposition against Black masculine norms, which may lead to strain in the parent-child relationship due to the parents' endorsed homonegative beliefs. Data highlights that same gender loving Black youth may even face the risk of familial ostracizing when they choose to embrace and express themselves in ways that juxtapose commonly accepted presentations of masculinity (Horn & Wong, 2014; Lasala & Frierson, 2012; Whiting & Lewis, 2008).

> I hear stories of friends of mine who've had relatively tragic relationships with their parents, as children, because of their perceived sexuality, and that wasn't necessarily the case for me. I probably came out to my parents, I was around 25, so not that long ago. The relationship is interesting. I guess it's one of acceptance. Since that day there's never been any other conversations, or questions—perhaps I guess if I was a straight male—you know, "How's dating going" or "Who are you talking to?" Because parents want to see their children happy in those ways. And so it's love and nothing has changed except for the unspoken part, which is a big part of me; so in many ways that's a little weird. They're getting some of me, or they *love* some of me, rather, but a big part is kind of left out. I think they think it's not a thing,

or they're okay with it being in the shadows, and that connects to this erasure. No one talks about it—now I'm speaking for my parents—I never have to leave this earth knowing I had a true gay son; but we didn't meet anybody, we didn't do any weddings. So, it serves this narrative of erasure. I don't get that there is an eagerness for me to fully live into that truth with them.

Simeon, 31, Brooklyn, NY

Being a Black man was, about not having emotion but being concerned about what people thought about you because, at least in my family, everything was about reputation. My mother's side of the family was very famous in the sports world, playing basketball and football. When it came to me not wanting to follow that, it made me feel like and outsider.

Devin, 25, Charleston, SC

In addition to struggling with their son's gender expressions, many parents of Black same gender loving men find difficulty in witnessing the intersectional oppressions their child may face due to their multiple marginalized identities (Lasala & Frierson, 2012). Coined by Kimberlé Crenshaw in 1989, intersectionality relates to the way marginalized identities can place an individual, or group, at risk of experiencing increased systemic oppression in comparison to those who are less marginalized. While this term was written specifically for the experiences of Black women, it's framework can be adopted to understand the experiences of Black same gender loving men. Unable to cope with the fear and anxieties that accompany the unknown social consequences of having a same gender loving Black son, some parents may psychically, emotionally, and mentally distance themselves from their sons (Lasala & Frierson, 2012). Research communicates that this rejection places Black same gender loving men at increased risk of experiencing various negative outcomes such as internalized homonegativity, which serves as a conduit to other negative health outcomes such as substance abuse, mental illness, poverty, and homelessness (Alexander, 2004; Amola & Grimmett, 2015; Choi, Paul, Ayala, Boylan, & Gregorich, 2013; Quinn et al., 2015; Rosario, Rotheram-Borus & Reid, 1996). Few studies address the ways that parent–child interactions influence romantic pairings among Black men, yet theories of attachment communicate that the parent–child bonds created—or in this case, not created—in youth can greatly impact interpersonal functioning in adulthood (Haydon et al., 2012; Stefanou & McCabe, 2012).

Clinician's corner

Some Black same gender loving male youth's difficulty (or resistance) to adhere to communal expectations of masculinity lead to both perceptions and experiences of being rejected by family members.

- What, in your opinion, does this dynamic say about the family members who reject their Black same gender loving youth?
- What are the areas that can be identified as points of intervention to reduce the prevalence of perceived and experienced rejection Black same gender loving men and boys experience by their familial environments?

Truth: It is time to dispel the myth of same gender loving identity being connected to absent Black fathers

A common misconception in the Black community is that Black same gender loving men are often raised without fathers or male figures to assist them in becoming "real men" (Jones & Mosher, 2013). Many additionally assume that being surrounded by women (i.e., mothers, aunts, sisters, grandmothers, and other female figures) influence same gender loving men to adopt "feminine behaviors" and, consequently, a same gender loving male identity (Grant, 2020a). These assumptions are disempowering the Black community on varying levels. The narrative of the absent or deadbeat Black father is a false trope that conflicts with data which highlights how a majority of Black fathers in the United States live with and raise their children; and it ignores the racist systems (e.g., the systems that overincarcerate Black men and limit their gainful employment) that keep some Black fathers away from their children (Alexander, 2010; 2012; Jones & Mosher, 2013). This lie-ridden narrative further ignores that the residence of Black fathers does not capture the involvement of Black fathers in their child's lives, as research presents that a greater percentage of Black fathers who do not live with their children are nevertheless heavily involved in their children's lives and influence traits and behaviors such as increased racial salience and pride, increased self-esteem, safe sexual engagement, and later onset of sexual activity (Allen, 2016; Hussen et al., 2014). Through this logic, it is probable that many Black same gender loving men and boys have some form of relationship with their fathers. What stands striking is that many Black same gender loving men still possess the capacity to sexually and romantically love other men when many of their experiences with their fathers have been documented to be laden with hypervigilance of behavioral expression, fear, rejection, regulation, conditional love, and violence (Fields et al., 2015; Horn & Wong, 2014; Savin-Williams, 1994). Many Black fathers perceive that it is their responsibility to teach their sons about how "to be men" (Allen, 2016). Literature suggests that Black manhood is shaped by salient themes such as self-determinism and accountability/responsibility, familial engagement, racial, cultural, and personal, pride, and spiritual engagement/leadership (Allen, 2016; Hunter & Davis, 1992; Whiting & Lewis, 2008). However, a shift in social values is reflected in the documented ways Black fathers are now promoting emotional availability, vulnerability, and expression in their heterosexual sons—traits that have been observed, yet socially repressed, among Black men throughout history (Allen, 2016). Yet this newly encouraged freedom of expression seems limited when it involves same gender loving sons. Qualitative reports note Black fathers' often physically and emotionally damaging attempts to overly indoctrinate their suspected same gender loving sons into masculine socialization (Monteiro, & Fuqua, 1993; Savin-Williams, 1994). Research presents Black same gender loving sons as recipients of rejection and physical, mental, and emotional abuse from their fathers, due to their same gender loving identity or atypical gender expression (Choi, Paul, Ayala, Boylan, & Gregorich, 2013; Savin-Williams, 1994). Literature suggests that such responses reflect Black fathers' own internalized homonegative views, internalized fears of their son's increased marginalization from the external world, internalized anxieties regarding potential negative health outcomes assumed to be connected to the same gender loving identity, and internalized judgments regarding their inability to "protect" their sons from having non-heterosexual sexual identities (Horn & Wong, 2014; Jadwin-Cakmak, Pingel, Harper, & Bauermeister, 2015; Lasala & Frierson, 2012; Savin-Williams, 1994; Rosario, Rotheram-Borus, & Reid, 1996). Such responses, however, do nothing to nurture the healthy development of Black same gender loving men and boys, and often serve as the initial influences of internalized homonegativity among Black same gender loving men and boys.

> When I was younger, I feel like I let my dad down. I wasn't the boy who wanted to play sports, or watch sports, or wanted to learn how to fix a certain part of the car; and I remember instances and experiences very vividly where I was over it. I was like, "I

know you're trying to do this thing—the ball and the mitt—and I don't want to do this."

David, 32, Charleston, SC

If something came on TV or the news, my dad would sometimes let the word, "fag" slip and every time he said it, it would hurt me because, little did he know, his own son was a part of that community. The only person in my family who I haven't opened up to is my father because I have such a good relationship with him. Though I know he won't disown me, I don't want to jeopardize the bond that he and I have. I know, as a father, he may feel let down because of his own perception and definition of what it means to be gay.

Edgar, 30, Lawnside, NJ

I don't think my dad will receive my identity well. I'm so nervous to tell him. I'm afraid it will completely rupture and damage our relationship. It goes back to this fear of me losing my dad—he won't take it well.

Chris, 30, Charlotte, NC

Truth: We can't ignore Black mothers' role in the perpetuation of homonegativity

It is interesting how overexposure to femininity has been used to explain the "cause" of Black same gender loving male identity (Fields, Bogart, Smith, & Malebranche, 2015). Socially constructed gender role stereotypes, often supported by empirical data, will lead us to believe that most Black fathers are disappointed by their son's same gender loving identity, and mothers are understanding and more likely to accept same gender loving sons. Research highlights how some Black mothers throughout the diaspora contrast Black fathers and wholly support, protect, and love their same gender loving male children, which influences others to accept the same gender loving youth (Soldati-Kahimbaara, 2016). Data also highlights Black mothers' active roles in further understanding the experiences of their same gender loving children, despite potentially being raised in homonegative environments (Soldati-Kahimbaara, 2016). However, increasing literature has taken a more balanced view and suggested that some Black mothers can be just as violent as Black fathers, if not more violent, against their same gender loving sons (D'Augelli, Grossman, & Starks, 2005; Horn & Wong, 2014; Moore et al., 2019).

Take, for example, City Girls rapper Caresha Brownlee (also known as Young Miami), who told her social media followers that she would physically assault her son if he identified as gay. Such violence from Black mothers toward their sons not only highlights another negative impact of familial homonegativity on Black same gender loving men; it highlights Black cisgender heterosexual (cis-het) women's contribution to the promotion of hegemonic Black male masculinity (Collins 2004; Whiting & Lewis, 2008). While Black cis-het women may enjoy Black same gender loving men as their beauticians, confidants, and other secondary roles, there seems to be a low tolerance for familial proximity to same gender loving identity (D'Augelli, Grossman, & Starks, 2005; Horn & Wong, 2014; Lasala & Frierson, 2012; Moore et al., 2019). The aversion to having a Black same gender loving child may further support findings of parental anxieties that arise when parents recognize the increased marginalization, and assumed negative health outcomes, their Black same gender loving sons may experience due to their diverse sexual identities and potential divergent gender expressions (Lasala & Frierson, 2012).

> When I came out to my parents, my mother was different. She got quiet and seemed to have been studying the conversation. Maybe it was violent, in a way; maybe it was a subtle resistance. She had questions like, "Are you sure? Did something happen to you when you were younger that made you think you were gay?" It was a subtle pushing back. My mom is more influenced by the perceptions of other people; I think she was like, "What will this mean for how people think of what I did to raise a son."
>
> Simeon, 31, Brooklyn, NY

> Anytime I showed something "not man-like" it was, "D, don't do that. Don't sit that way" or "Don't sing that song. Don't talk like this. Don't wear that." Things like that. I remember I was watching a movie—it was *Drumline*— and I was imitating the dancers. And she saw it, called me in the room, and had that *real hard* conversation. "Why are you dancing like that? What are you doing? Do you want to be a girl?" That alone, and the look on her face, really scared the shit out of me; I was just having fun.
>
> Devin, 25, Charleston, SC

I was molested as a child by a family friend, who was a Black male. That was my introduction to same sex anything. After sharing that with my mother, I think she leverages that experience. And that's one of the negatives; that I keep getting reminded of the things that happened to me, which I had no control over, as the reason for why I identify how I identify.

MJ, 30, Charlotte, NC

The biggest takeaway that can be offered by observing the experiences of Black same gender loving men and their parents is that same gender loving men cannot be held responsible for being harmed by parental homonegative reactions to same gender loving identity. Accountability must be directed toward the parents and the systems, which influence homonegative beliefs, fears related to same gender loving identity and atypical gender expressions, and negative perceptions of what it means to be a Black same gender loving man.

7 Navigating Homonegativity in Schools and Workplaces

As a first-generation Jamaican American who possessed limited knowledge about navigating the American college application system, paying for higher education in a recession, and understanding the differences between education at a Historically Black College or University (HBCU) versus a predominantly white institution (pwi), I am surprised that I identified the fraternity of my dreams early in my collegiate career. I witnessed a group of men—members of a Black Greek Letter Fraternity/Organization (BGLF/O)—who were leaders on campus and in their respective fields, and I saw myself aligned in values, aspirations, and deeds. However, when I finally mustered the courage to express interest in fraternal life, I perceived two things disqualifying me from relationship with these gentlemen—my budding same gender loving identity that was paired with an uninhibited feminine gender expression. Although unofficially "out" on my predominantly white college campus, I heard of the presumed intolerance for same gender loving identity and expression that colored Greek affiliation, as the relatively small Black community, at the time, cycled rumors of a fraternal aspirant who dropped line (i.e., withdrew his application into the organization) due to inquiries regarding his same gender loving proclivities. At that moment, anxiety and internalized homonegativity told me that pursing this organization was a lost cause.

Two years after graduating from undergrad, I perceived myself as having unfinished business with my dream fraternity and I decided to aspire toward membership at the graduate level. Unsurprisingly, the homonegativity I feared as an undergraduate resurfaced to a greater extent on the alumni level. As an official initiate, I endured inquiries and rumors surrounding my sexual and romantic orientation and gender identity, and opposition to my membership before, during, and after my initiation. What stood further perplexing—traumatizing—was the

DOI: 10.4324/9781003180937-8

existence I navigated once I became a Brother; an existence that was verbally rejected and nonverbally adored, demonized through rumor and fetishized through social media, publicly distanced and privately worshipped. In this book, I have presented homonegativity in the religious and familial spheres. Yet as I exist as a veteran in both the realms of academia and fraternal life, I find necessity to explore the ways homonegativity, femmephobia, and hegemonic masculinity shape the experiences of Black men in their educational journeys, fraternal pursuits, and professional navigations.

Truth: The familial message of normative male behavior is learned at home and reinforced by peer interactions

Black male youth often learn what presentations reflect manhood, early in their lifespans, from familial spaces, religious spheres, and through social group interactions (Griffin, 2010; hooks, 2004; Lemelle, 2010; Whiting & Lewis, 2008). Before they begin to acknowledge same gender loving sexual and romantic attraction, many Black same gender loving men struggle to navigate early peer spaces, as they are often identified by peers as having atypical male presentations (Downs, 2005; Grant, 2020b; Pascoe, 2011). Such presentation includes having proclivities for academics and female companionship, rather than desires to engage with boys through sports or other tasks assigned masculine (Grant, 2020b; Pascoe, 2011). Some youth have experiences of being preemptively identified as same gender loving through their expression of artistic abilities or quiet temperaments (Downs, 2005; Grant, 2020b; Pascoe, 2011). Regardless of the variables linking Black male youth to perceived same gender loving identity, what continues to stand salient is the limited scope with which Black boyhood and manhood is measured. The traits given enslaved people—traits of baseness, inhibited aggressive expression, and physical prowess—have become markers that denote Black male youth in-group affiliation (hooks, 2004; Nederveen Pieterse, 1992; Slatton & Spates, 2014; 2016); and those who fall outside these molds often learn to adapt their behaviors to gain social acceptance, or risk navigating childhood and adulthood with experiences of bullying and social ostracization.

I have been bullied by guys and girls in the school setting because I was too feminine. At the time I didn't understand the word gay or the word faggot, I just thought these people were calling me names. I got beat up by a girl once and that didn't help at all; that really messed up my self-esteem growing up. In middle school I didn't have more than three friends. There were people who wanted to be friends with me, but they were so consumed by the masculinity that they didn't want to be gay by association.

Devin, 25, Charleston, SC

I was a smart kid but, for a lot of people from where I was, being smart was seen as "being white." My brother wanted to play sports; I like studying rocks and animals. Being a male had its challenges because I was more feminine than a lot of guys around me. All those comments weigh on you—I think that definitely had an impact on every decision I wanted to make as a kid, a teenager, even going into college; whether that was what major I wanted to be in or what extracurriculars I wanted to do. I was hindered because of those comments.

Rammy, 30, Wilson, NC

What's your truth?

- Can you recall a story of someone you know who was teased for "being gay" while you were growing up (this person can be you or someone else)?
- What happened to that person during that time? How bad did the teasing get?
- What impact do you think the teasing had on that individual?
- What would you say to that person today?

Truth: Homonegativity often prevents Black same gender loving men in higher education from fully participating in institutions intended to uplift Black folx

Although research readily presents the homonegativity Black same gender loving men may endure in familial and religious spaces, there remains scarce and unclear literature regarding the ways Black same gender loving men navigate and engage with homonegativity in educational environments (Ford, 2015; Lemelle, 2010; Pitt, 2009; Strayhorn, Blakewood, & DeVita, 2008; Strayhorn & Tillman-Kelly, 2013). Investigative studies communicate that after navigating same gender loving identities with family and religion, Black same gender loving youth who pursue secondary education may seek enrollment at institutions that will perceivably compensate for the lack of support experienced previously (Strayhorn, Blakewood, & DeVita, 2008; Strayhorn & Tillman-Kelly, 2013). Some Black same gender loving men have viewed Historically Black Colleges and Universities (HBCUs) as havens that will aid them in experiencing more affirming social interactions. However, literature suggests that the historical conservative and moralistic values that shape and permeate HBCU institutions counterbalance—through the reinforcing of traditional gender roles and hegemonic masculinities—the support many Black same gender loving men anticipate receiving in these arenas (Ford, 2015; Mendoza-Denton, Downey, Purdie, Davis, & Pietrzak, 2002; Strayhorn & Tillman-Kelly, 2013). HBCU institutions however are microcosms of the Black community, in which Black same gender loving presence and community is apparent, available, and becoming more visible for Black men seeking spaces that will nurture and affirm their same gender loving identities.

The experience of Black same gender loving men at predominantly white institutions presents as more complex, as Black same gender loving men must navigate marginalization due to their race and same gender loving identities (Totten, 2015). Research provides that the broader social stereotypes of Black men being violent, criminal, uncivilized, and unintelligent often follow them into predominantly white collegiate institutions, and often impact attrition and academic performance rates (Dancy, 2011a; Goode-Cross & Tager, 2011; Travers, 2019). Such hostile academic environments will often motivate *homosociality* (i.e., intimate yet platonic bonding between individuals of the same sex) among Black men seeking community with individuals of the same race (Hui & Jackson, 2017). These connections not only provide opportunities for resisting the racist forces present in predominantly white academic institutions; they afford Black men the opportunity to share in emotional vulnerability, and create familial bonds, with other men. Research highlights how within this homosociality exists a form of Black masculinity that resists the white supremacist image of Black manhood—an image that presents Black men as emotionally unavailable, physically aggressive, sexually insatiable, and socially degenerate—and embraces an Afrocentric form of masculinity that is focused on individual and communal upliftment, emotional availability, and intellectual and mental soundness (Hui & Jackson, 2017; McGuire, Berhanu, Davis, & Harper, 2014; Pelzer, 2016). Such deviations from white constructions of Black masculinity position fraternal bonding as an important aspect of collegiate life for many Black men.

The first intercollegiate Black Greek Letter Fraternity/Organization (BGLF/O) was created on the campus of Cornell University in Ithaca, New York in 1906 (Ross, 2008). This organization was created with the intention to nurture Black men, throughout the collegiate process, at a time in which Black male college enrollment was severely impacted by the social and structural resistance that arose in newly integrated college institutions (Hughey, Parks, & Skocpol, 2011). Over time, one organization inspired the creation of other Black Greek Letter Fraternities and Sororities and there now stands five incorporated Black Greek Letter Fraternities—Alpha Phi Alpha, Fraternity, Inc., Kappa Alpha Psi, Fraternity, Inc., Omega Psi Phi, Fraternity, Inc., Phi Beta Sigma, Fraternity, Inc., and Iota Phi Theta, Fraternity, Inc. These organizations have established an international legacy focused on building the Black community through ideals such as scholarship and social awareness. Membership in a Black Greek Letter Organization has served as a historical marker of one who possesses prominence in the Black community (Graham, 1999). This prominence reflects W.E.B. Du Bois' (1903) assertion that a "talented tenth" in the Black community—those who were educated, possessed high ranking careers, and positive social standing—would be responsible for uplifting the entire Black community. Years after Du Bois' assertion, many who identified as the "talented tenth" also possessed membership in a Black Greek Letter organization. However, over generations, expectation of the Black community's progression being contingent on an elite sect made room for the proliferation of other white supremacist tools and ideologies within Black Greek Letter Organizations, including homonegativity.

Never will it be erroneously suggested that Black same gender loving men do not assume significant space in Black Greek Letter Organizations. Yet initiation and membership are made difficult for Black men—same gender loving and heterosexual alike—who are unable or unwilling to perform Black masculinity in ways that adhere to the expectations of Black masculinities outlined by white supremacy (DeSantis & Coleman, 2008). Research details the benefits often gained by Black men who join Black Greek Letter Organizations, such as increased community, social networking, increased exposure to community involvement, and the ability to bond emotionally with other Black men—Afrocentric ideals that were stripped and distorted through colonialism (Dancy, 2011b; Jenkins,

2012; McClure, 2006). However, research also denotes a fraternal adherence to traditional and hegemonic masculinities within Black Greek Letter Organizations that often promotes the barring of same gender loving men—confirmed or suspected—from the fraternal space (DeSantis & Coleman, 2008; Jones, 2015; McClure, 2006). Many male members of Black Greek Letter Organizations believe in the preservation of the "real Black man" and endorse the pathological belief of the endangered Black man (Jones, 2015; McClure, 2006). To many members, same gender loving Black men are not real men. They are men who have the potential to become sexually or romantically attracted to other men in the fraternal space; they are men who juxtapose the moralistic precepts on which Black Greek Letter Organizations were founded. Black same gender loving men in fraternal spaces also incite fears within some heterosexual men that they may become victim to the same misogyny and hegemonic masculinity they enact upon women. Black same gender loving men who seek membership into Black Greek Letter Organizations may find themselves having to separate themselves from any portrayal of same gender loving identity or feminine affect whilst under fraternal scrutiny (Ford, 2015; Totten, 2015). Further, even after becoming initiated into their aspired organizations, many Black same gender loving men continue to shroud their identities—by avoiding public sexual and romantic contact with other men and heightening their performances of masculinity—for fear of losing social capital within the Greek space, due to their same gender loving identities.

> I pursued Greek life and got to the point where it was time to cross, and I pulled back. I wasn't comfortable crossing because I felt I would have been stuck to act a certain in way or be forced to act like a heterosexual male; and I would bring shame upon myself if I was the opposite and lost that sense of community.
>
> Justin, 30, Cleveland, OH

> Once I was well into my organization, I had the privilege of bringing in some members. During that time, and even after, I found myself having to fight for individuals who identified as Black and queer, or who may have presented themselves on the more feminine side of the spectrum. I was fighting the fights—talking down to bigotry, nonsense, and silliness; trying to help people see a different side of the coin. I don't regret it. And it's not all like that, but I think it's a mirror of other experiences I've had

in the Black community.

Marcus, 35, Clifton, MD

Navigating my sexual identity in Greek life can be confusing. On one hand you have some of men who are like, "This is wrong." On the other hand, you have men who are just hidden with it. They put on this masculine energy in a meeting but outside of that they're trying to pursue men. In my mind, it's a sense of confusion.

Devin, 25, Charleston, SC

We're so busy trying to survive that we don't allow ourselves the privilege of space to thrive. While we could have a conversation about same gender loving people in Black Greek spaces, we must also converse about community service, actual impact, violence against women, and the intake process. There are always one thousand things going on and, partially because of these compounded things and because we allow ourselves to cop out, we allow the status quo to remain how we operate. We get shut down by motherfuckers who say, "Nope, it's different, it's not how I was raised to be. It's not what I was told Greek life was." Which is, of course, antithetical to the entire brand and concept of many organizations. But I think that space operates as a microcosm of the Black community at large.

Xavier, 32, Philadelphia, PA

Truth: For Black same gender loving men, codeswitching is an intersectional issue

Extending beyond the homonegativity found in secondary education are the behaviors that are observed when Black same gender loving men's internalization of homonegativity follow them after college. While few investigations have detailed the experiences of Black same gender loving men in the workplace, studies highlight that Black and non-Black same gender loving men may seek to avoid performances and expressions they perceive may highlight or disclose their same sex attracted identities (Rumens & Kerfoot, 2009; Rumens, 2010). Narrative based literature communicates that regardless of how affirming a work environment may be of same gender loving identity, same gender loving men's hypervigilance of the socially heteronormative and hegemonically masculine expectations existing in the workplace may restrict them from expressing behaviors that perceivably challenge these norms (such as identity disclosure, friendship formation with gay men, and behavioral displays that may be associated with queerness or femininity) (Griffith & Hebl, 2002; Rumens & Kerfoot, 2009; Rumens, 2010). This behavior is not solely characteristic of Black same gender loving men who are closeted or uncomfortable with their sexual and romantic attractions. Research suggests that some—arguably all—Black men are aware of the social systems that marginalize Black folx (Grant, 2020b). This awareness, which stems from living in the Black community, understanding Black history, adopting a Black communal pride, and experiencing the oppressions that result from living in a racist system, has conditioned some Black men to navigate life in a manner that reduces the risk of experienced oppression. For some Black men, owning a same gender loving identity in the workplace stands as an additional "strike" to social and professional status, and may place them at risk for increased workplace discrimination. There is validity in this stance, as before June of 2020, Black same gender loving men risked losing their employment and professional status due to race and sexual and romantic attraction (Grant, 2020).[1]

Due to this awareness, some Black same gender loving men choose to engage in racial and gendered codeswitching—a form of changing behavior and affect in a specific environment in order to align more closely with the majority (Grant, 2020b). Codeswitching allows for Black same gender loving men to mask their same sexual and romantic orientations, despite being unable to hide the color of their skin. Some Black same gender loving men employ this homonegativity-fueled professional play in order to minimize their risk of intersectional marginalization. Even in spaces in which these men may be perceived by their coworkers to be same gender loving, codeswitching, adherence to respectability politics, and heightened masculine performance foster an environment that removes any opportunity to discuss same gender sexual and romantic attraction in the workplace (Grant, 2020b). This behavioral navigation is so effective in helping Black same gender loving men avoid confronting their identities, some men may perceive same gender recognition and affirmation at work as irrelevant to their job satisfaction and performance (Grant, 2020b).

> I am the Black person, I guess, my coworkers can be around, and they don't feel afraid, they feel safe. To play into codeswitching,

there's diction, articulation in speech, a pleasantness and kindness in my tone that I think fits the mold of the employee they want to staff. Maybe I see codeswitching as placating the circles you're in. If in a circle where the other parties are heterosexual and more masculine, you compartmentalize your sexual orientation. It is there but it's in the small bag. If you're around your girlfriends, then you're carrying a medium sized tote of your sexual orientation. You do what you need to.

David, 32, Charleston, SC

As research acknowledges the impact of all identities on functioning in professional settings, the minimizing of same gender loving identity suggests that some Black same gender loving men—in not understanding how to safely navigate their sexual and romantic identities in the workplace—may stunt themselves by constructing professional environments in which their identities are unable to be acknowledged or discussed (Grant, 2020b; Pedulla, 2014).

Truth: Some perceive same gender loving identity to be a professional privilege

Those who attempt to argue against the phenomenon of homonegativity, and its impact on the lives of Black same gender loving men in the professional sphere, have recently propagated homonegativity by promoting the concept of Black same gender loving male privilege. Instead of positioning same gender loving identity as a factor that positions one to experience increased marginalization in the workspace, some have suggested that Black same gender loving men are more advantaged than their heterosexual counterparts, as their sexual orientation (which becomes conflated by the majority with feminine gender identity) counters their Black and male identities (Grant, 2020b). Many have argued that Black same gender loving men have an easier time navigating and succeeding in majority white professional and educational spaces, as their same gender loving identity allows them to adopt the trope of the magical, refined, noble Negro, who takes pleasure in aiding white protagonists (i.e., peers, bosses, corporations) in obtaining success. Studies have supported this phenomenon by highlighting how many Black same gender loving men hold high positions in education, medicine, business, media, entertainment, and other professional industries (Fitz, 2015; Jones, 2015).

Research has also suggested that Black same gender loving male privilege appears in the ways Black same gender loving men are compensated in the workplace. Pedulla's (2014) study, which investigated the ways different demographic groups may be compensated in the workplace, suggests that employers will often offer Black same gender loving men salaries comparable to those offered to white heterosexual men. These salaries were noted to surpass offers given to heterosexual Black men and white gay men. However, to collude with Pedulla (2014) in using entry salary as a marker of Black same gender loving male privilege would be to ignore the other factors that may contribute to these outcomes. The intersectional marginalization Black same gender loving men experience due to their race and sexual orientations often influences their professional and educational investment and advancement, which positions them as highly qualified candidates in professional spaces (Downs, 2005; Grant, 2020b). Additionally, if research accurately represents Black same gender loving male experiences, lifelong navigation of homonegative spaces may equip Black same gender loving men with a developed hypervigilance that influences stellar work performance, in order to avoid negative critique, and the resilience and negotiation skills to demand better professional benefits. While these traits may seem beneficial to the professional progress of Black same gender loving men, such traits have their origins in homonegativity and often do not protect Black men from racial oppressions they may experience in the professional sphere.

> My life at work can be isolating. Being young, Black, same gender loving in a space that is majority older, and white, and majority not same gender loving. It's interesting to say the perception that I'm same gender loving is more accepted; and I think that stems from the idea that same gender loving people aren't confrontational—it disarms people, particularly as a Black man. And I find that people rarely view them together; they are together but based on the situation, or what their aims are for the interaction, will lean to one more. If I am communicating a grievance or pinpointing something that was racialized, in that conversation people could then only see my Blackness, or they'll stick with that because there's a long history of how Black people are treated and gaslit. They'll then engage with me like I'm a Black person in a white space; and for that purpose, me being same gender loving doesn't need to be in the formula.
>
> Simeon, 31, Brooklyn, NY

What's your truth?

• What are your thoughts about Black same gender loving male privilege?
• How do you regard a privilege that is based on the reduction of Blackness due to same gender loving status?

Note

1 On June 15, 2020, the Supreme Court ruled to legally protect lesbian, gay, bisexual, and transgender (LGBT) people from workplace discrimination (Liptak, 2020).

8 The Internal Manifestations of Homonegativity

Truth: Shame serves as the mediator between external and internalized homonegativity among Black same gender loving men

At its simplest conceptualization, shame has been defined as negative thoughts and affect one holds toward their being (i.e., "I am flawed") (Dorahy et al., 2012, 2013). Literature has expanded upon this description to position shame as the experienced tension between who we are and who we wish to be; the negative sentiments and perceived inferiority we adapt when we regard ourselves as unable to live up to a set of established norms; and the negative appraisals we endorse after enduring a traumatic event (Dorahy et al., 2012, 2013; Gilbert & Miles, 2000; Mantzoukas et al., 2021). Marsha Linehan (2009), in her clinical work with patients who experienced various traumas and expressed features of borderline personality disorder, identifies shame as a learned response to existing in invalidating environments (i.e., environments that communicate and reinforce the inappropriateness of an individual's thoughts, feelings, and existence), and a maintaining factor for emotional dysregulation and impaired interpersonal functioning. Systems of white superiority have forced Black folxs into compounded, shame-filled, trauma experiences which have taught many in the Black community to view shame as a tool that can coerce others into adhering to social norms (Beam, 2008; Johnson, 2014; Collins, 2004; hooks, 2004; Schwarz, 2003; Snorton, 2014; Tennial, 2015). However, Tanya Denise Fields reminds us that, "shame doesn't course correct … shame is a liar, a thief, a murderer of dreams and vision. Shame is a manipulator" (Burke & Brown, 2021).

DOI: 10.4324/9781003180937-9

What's the difference between shame and guilt?

Research has sought to investigate the difference between shame and guilt, as it relates to mood and functioning. Guilt involves negative feelings toward a committed action that contrasts one's values, whereas shame captures negative feelings toward one's being, absent of committed action (Dorahy et al. 2013). Whereas shame keeps an individual in states of rumination and negative affect, the negative feelings of guilt are sometimes effective in correcting unwanted or undesired behavior.

The various conceptualizations of shame capture the undercurrent of Black same gender loving men's experiences with internalized homonegativity. Internalized homonegativity stands the shame-driven negative appraisals and perceived inferiorities (e.g., decreased social ranking) Black same gender loving men endorse when they recognize how their sexual and romantic identities juxtapose the social norms of masculinity presented by family, religion, peers, and other institutions (Grant, 2020b). Internalized homonegativity convinces Black same gender loving men that their sexual and romantic attractions are the causes of their sexual and social victimization, and it further primes them for revictimization in diverse settings (Gilbert & Miles, 2000; Grant, 2020). Internalized homonegativity does not improve Black same gender loving men's lives by assisting them in performing masculinity; it kills the spirit, creates cognitive dissonance, impacts Black same gender loving male functioning, and negatively impacts Black same gender loving male quality of life across the lifespan.

Adverse childhood experiences (ACEs)

When you're a kid you don't really know what type of different people exist. You just know you're a kid, and things are fun, and things look pretty, that's it. So, when you're four or five and you hear your babysitter, or the person that's supposed to be your caretaker, tell your parents, "Hey, your son is gay. You might want to fix that." That's the first negative experience I had regarding my sexuality and that was probably the first experience that made me realize that I couldn't be the kid that I wanted to be, or could be.

Rammy, 30, Wilson, NC

From 1995 to 1997, the Centers for Disease Control and Prevention and Kaiser Permanente (inspired by decades-long research on negative childhood experiences) explored how childhood abuse and neglect, parental divorce, and household violence increased the risk of adulthood mortality and morbidity outcomes (Van der Feltz-Cornelis, 2018, 2019). Research has found that childhood bullying and low parental support due to sexual orientation are Adverse Childhood Experiences(ACEs) that, when compounded and chronic in exposure, can be conceptualized as complex traumas that can lead to complex PTSD (Fuller-Thomson, Baird, Dhrodia, & Brennenstuhl, 2016; Idsoe et al., 2020; 2021). Complex PSTD is described as a relational disorder that stems from relational trauma. When a Black same gender loving man is shamed, bullied, and ostracized for their sexual and romantic attractions, or primed to believe that same gender loving identity is unnatural and deviant, he is conditioned in relational trauma, which leads to experiences of shame and shame response outcomes (e.g., isolation, low trust in relationships, difficulty establishing same gender platonic and sexual relationships, feelings of unworthiness, desires to conform to majority beliefs and behaviors) (Dorahy et al., 2012; 2013; Gilbert & Miles, 2000). Chronic and compounded Adverse Childhood and Adolescent Events (CAEs and AAEs)—such as in-person, cyber, or perceived childhood, adolescent, and early adult bullying; homonegative rhetoric during religious services; physical, verbal, mental, and emotional degradation from family members due to perceived or confirmed same gender loving status—serve as complex traumas that influence Black same gender loving men to blame themselves for their experienced mistreatment, and condition negative self-appraisals related to same gender loving identity (Dorahy et al., 2012; 2013; Fuller-Thomson, Baird, Dhrodia, & Brennenstuhl, 2016; Gilbert & Miles, 2000; Idsoe et al., 2020; 2021; Mersky, Topitzes, & Reynolds, 2013). Many of the Black same gender loving men I have interviewed throughout my work identified that their consistent exposure to homonegative environments influenced shame-filled self-perceptions of being flawed, less of a man, unworthy, unattractive, and not fully integrated into the Black community (Grant, 2020b).

Truth: The outcomes of internalized homonegativity among SGL Black men go beyond HIV/AIDS

I was bullied by classmates, siblings, and cousins. It would be physical, verbal, and emotional. Being called faggot, gay, a girl, really took a toll on me during childhood. In high school it kind of went away, but it was still apparent that people had their assumptions about me. I felt like I didn't have a safe place, so there were moments I'd just go in my corner when no one was around, or just go in the backyard and just cry; and then come back and just be the man I was told I needed to be.

Devin, 25, Charleston, SC

Meyer (2003) first introduced minority stress theory to depict how various systems of oppression contribute to negative health outcomes for many sexual minorities. According to Meyer (1995; 2003), "prejudice and stigma directed to [same gender loving folx] bring about unique stressors ... and these stressors cause adverse health outcomes ... [including] mental and physical disorders." Much of the present literature that excavates Black same gender loving male lived experiences solely investigate their lives in connection to HIV/AIDS prevention and research (Frost, Lehavot, & Meyer, 2015). Although internalized homonegativity has been documented to influence Black same gender loving men's engagement in sexually risky behaviors, which contribute to the rising rates of HIV/AIDS and other infections within this cohort, consistently shaping the lives of Black same gender loving men through HIV/AIDS prevention and research perpetuates a systematically constructed narrative in which Black same gender loving men remain the face of HIV/AIDS (Carrillo & Hoffman, 2018; Quinn & Dickinson-Gomez, 2015; Quinn et al., 2015; Shoptaw et al., 2009). Further, narrowly focusing on the causes and prevalence of "risky behavior" among Black same gender loving men without exploring the holistic experiences of this cohorts strips Black same gender loving men of their humanity (Kaminski, 2008). It is necessary that the following message be emphasized for clinicians, researchers, and any professionals who engage in work with Black same gender loving men—Black same gender loving men are human. Scientific study and research have historically positioned Black people, Black men, and Black same gender loving men as objects for scientific advancement (as evidenced by the Tuskegee Experiment, the experience of Henritta Lax, and the systemic positioning of Black same gender loving men as the forefront of the HIV/AIDS epidemic). However, Black people—Black same gender loving men—are people who have expressed natural human responses to the lifespan oppressions they have endured.

Clinician's corner

In addition to rapport building and exploring your same gender loving clients' history, quantitative measures may provide greater understanding of their experiences. Here are some measures that can assist clinicians in assessing adult same gender loving clients' internalized homonegativity, depression and anxiety symptoms, and experiences of minority stress (Balsam, Molina, Beadnell, Simoni, & Walters, 2011; Beck, 1996; Leary, 1983; Maggiora Vergano, Lauriola, & Speranza, 2015; Mayfield, 2001):

- Complex Trauma Questionnaire
- Internalized Homonegativity Inventory (IHNI)
- The LGBT People of Color Microaggressions Scale
- Beck Depression Inventory-II
- Brief Fear of Negative Evaluation Scale

The research, to date, on rates of depression and anxiety among Black same gender loving men (unrelated to HIV/AIDS) is obscure. However, the Trevor Project (2020) reported that 53% of Black same gender loving youth endorsed experiences with anxiety; 63% of Black same gender youth experienced depressive symptoms; and 44% of Black same gender loving youth considered dying by suicide in the past year (Meyer, 2015). These outcomes have been connected to experiences of familial and social rejection and other traumas, as exemplified through the life of Nigel Shelby, a 15-year-old same gender loving Black boy who died by suicide after living with depression and being a target of school bullying due to his sexual orientation (Griffith, 2019; Lasala & Frierson, 2012; Meyer, 2015; The Trevor Project, 2020). The negative cognitive and emotional experiences of Black same gender loving youth often persist across the lifespan (Grant, 2020b). Many Black same gender loving men have reported that their encounters with shame-driven internalized homonegativity have often led to poor mental health outcomes (Meyer, 2015; Wang et al., 2018). Black same gender loving men have endorsed low mood, irritability, low self-esteem/self-worth, isolation from loved ones, fears of how their same gender sexual and romantic attractions would impact their relationships and social ranking, hypervigilance of gender performance in various spaces, and fear of being uncovered as same gender loving (Grant, 2020b; Wang et al., 2018). These accounts arise from the chronic cognitive dissonance experienced when Black same gender loving men are unable to fully come into, express, and affirm, their identities (Barnes & Meyer, 2012).

Truth: It's time to talk about suicidality among Black same gender loving men

> When I would go to school, I was bullied for my perceived sexuality at the time. I would sit at the lunch table with my then friends. They would get up, move, and then they would walk by and call me a faggot. I remember that it was the worst feeling in the world. And I would just sit there and smile and just eat my food alone. There were times when I was younger where I did not want to be here anymore; and I had to fight through those thoughts.
>
> Julius, 33, Lumberton, NJ

Suicidal ideation, attempt, and completion are impacting Black same gender loving men across the lifespan. O'Donnell, Meyer, and Schwartz (2011) recently noted an increase in the amount of suicide attempts among Black same gender loving men; and Shain (2019) expanded upon this work by highlighting how increased suicidality was also present among Black same gender loving adolescents (Dube et al., 2001). Linehan (1993) marks suicide and nonsuicidal self-injury (NSSI) as a perceived effective way of reducing suffering when other options to regulate emotions, and reduce pain caused by adverse events, have been proved ineffective (Dube et al., 2001). Qualitative data from Black same gender loving men communicate that suicide also serves as a mechanism to keep Black same gender loving men from having to face the feared outcomes of their same gender loving sexual and romantic identities being questioned or disclosed in various settings (Grant, 2020b).

> I absolutely contemplated suicide when I was younger. There was a point—and this ties to the negative—after I was essentially blacklisted from joining a fraternity and one of my best friends who was already a brother in the organization came to me on the side and was like, "You are never going to get the votes because the higher-ups have already blacklisted you because they *think* you're gay." At that point I had never said anything out loud—had never done anything. Nobody had witnessed anything. But because I wasn't undeniably straight in their eyes, I was a liability. And so, like that was sort of just the, like, proverbial straw that kind of tipped it all over the edge.
>
> (Grant, 2020b)

Black same gender loving men's relationship to suicide further clarifies conceptualizations of external homonegativity, complex trauma, shame, internalized homonegativity, and behavioral outcomes. The messages

Black same gender loving men received from their external environments influence internal perceptions of decreased social ranking, inferiority, and an inability to meet masculine norms due to their sexual and romantic attractions. These internalized appraisals negatively impact mood and illicit fears around the consequences of sexual and romantic identity disclosure. Once these men must confront their fears of being outed (through social engagements, familial inquiries, or some other form of social navigation), some Black same gender loving men are placed in a "fight, flight, or freeze" scenario in which they perceive suicide as a viable form of avoidance.

What's your truth?

Having passive thoughts of "not wanting to be here" is common, especially when one is experiencing low mood or high stress and anxiety. There, however, is a difference between occasionally "not wanting to be here" and actively thinking about or planning one's departure from this world.

- What is your experience with low mood, anxiety, or suicidal ideation?
- What was happening in your life when you experienced low mood, anxiety, or suicidal ideation?
- How does reflecting on your experience impact the ways you view the experiences had by Black same gender loving men?

9 External Manifestations of Internalized Homonegativity

The impacts of internalized homonegativity do not end with experiences of negative thoughts, emotions, or suicidality. From a cognitive-behavioral standpoint, negative emotionality and cognition ultimately lead to behavioral dysfunction (Beck, 2011). It is therefore unsurprising that Black same gender loving men who experience shame and internalized homonegativity will also display maladaptive behaviors in response to their internalized homonegativity. Some Black same gender loving men will outwardly engage in heteronormative, hegemonic, and homophobic rhetoric and behavior—observed through verbal and physical gay bashing, degradation of women, and proclaimed heterosexuality—in order to perceivably increase social ranking and avoid the anticipated rejection that may accompany public sexual identity disclosure (Ford, 2015; hooks, 2004; McCune, 2008). Some Black same gender loving men become so tied to hegemonic script adherence that they may avoid engaging in friendships or romantic partnerships with feminine presenting Black men (Ford, 2015; Snorton, 2014). These behaviors, when unmanaged, may even lead some Black same gender loving men to engage in various forms of violence against men perceived as more feminine performing or presenting (Grant, 2020b). Although positioned as methods of social survival, these behaviors are directly linked to internalized homonegativity (Ford, 2015; Lemelle, 2010; McCune, 2008; Snorton, 2014). Such behaviors further hinder many Black same gender loving men from engaging in platonic and romantic relationships that may expand their spheres of social support (Edwards, 2016; Pitt, 2010; Totenhagen, Randall, & Lloyd, 2018). It is with this knowledge that the present chapter will explore the behavioral aspects of internalized homonegativity through the lens of hegemonic conformity.

DOI: 10.4324/9781003180937-10

Truth: Hegemonic masculinity makes no room for fats or femmes

In order to quell the cognitive dissonance that arises when one recognizes themselves as same gender loving in a heterosexist world, some Black same gender loving men will make efforts to align themselves as closely as possible to hegemonic norms. As highlighted in previous chapters, such hegemony may be perpetuated by heightening one's performance of masculinity or separating oneself from men who seemingly perform femininely, to reduce the risk of being labeled same gender loving by association. Qualitative reports highlight how same gender loving Black men have sought to avoid being labeled same gender loving by evading platonic relationships with feminine-performing men or by highlighting the femininity expressed by those men.

> I had one friend and I told him, when we first met, I was afraid of being his friend because I felt like the world perceived him as gay and I did not want to be a target. I was like, "No, I don't want to deal with that." But getting to know him, he's really cool. I apologized to him. I said, "I know getting to know me was very rough, but I was dealing with my own issues, my own internal conflicts, and I'm sorry for that. I wish that at the time I was able to see you as the great person that you are in front of me right now. However, I perceived you as not a bad guy, but not as something I could be around, because I wasn't comfortable with how people would perceive me."—which they were already perceiving me that way. So, pretty much, that all boiled down to, "I did not want to be cool with you because I was not comfortable with myself." But I was honest with him to tell him that after the fact, but that took some years of processing. I probably missed out on some other great friendships earlier in my life because of that.
>
> Julius, 33, Lumberton, NJ

This manner of navigating masculinity is so pervasive that it also impacts the type of man many Black same gender loving men seek to engage sexually and romantically, and often positions men who present or perform femininity as generally undesirable (Han, 2015; Reynolds, 2015). Same gender loving dating apps are often decorated with "masculine (masc) men seeking the same," or men who make clear that they aren't looking for "fats or femmes" (Reynolds, 2015). While possessing sexual or romantic preferences is not inherently negative, there exists utility in investigating the homonegative and hegemonic origins of said preferences (Totenhagen, Randall, & Lloyd, 2018). The hegemonic masculinity that reinforces internalized homonegativity among Black men has made "no fats, no femmes" an internal standard of desirability for many same gender loving Black men. Some Black men have identified that metrics around body shape, penis size, and sexual positioning are used to measure desirability in Black and non-Black folx, which reinforces the practice of assessing Black masculinity based on physical features (a tradition rooted in practices of enslavement and white supremacy). And while there is a contextual history of physique signifying health status during the HIV epidemic, physical prowess and strong physique also serve as a hegemonic marker of masculine appeal for many Black same gender loving men.

Black same gender loving men have been nurtured in systems of hegemony that position Black masculinity as strong, savage, angry yet emotionless, sexually insatiable, and physically supreme. Put plainly, Black men have been caricatured as eroticized superbeings. Hegemonic masculinity posits that same gender loving identity bars a Black man from achieving the fullness of Black masculinity. With this logic, many same gender loving Black men sexually and romantically idealize men who align more closely to the hegemonic ideal (Grant, 2020b). Some Black same gender loving men, attempting to separate their preferences from internalized homonegativity, have reported that engaging with a hegemonically masculine performing partner increases their comfort during public social engagement (Grant, 2020b). However, other Black same gender loving men have explicitly identified that pursuing men who display proximity to idealized masculinity exemplifies their discomfort around engaging with (and potentially being dominated by) a man who might be classified as feminine (Grant, 2020b).

> There have also been some people where I was like, "I did not realize that I was attracted to you as much as I was when I sat down and interrogated it." I had written it off earlier because it was like, "Oh, you are more feminine than I am and I already think I am queen enough." So anything more feels like ... too much, perhaps? And then, do you look or feel like the type of guy who I should allow to "take me" in this regard? I've been trying to interrogate that and figure out how to unlearn that. While at the same time falling for certain people and realizing that's also just who I'm attracted to; and they still fit certain masculine molds.
> Xavier, 33, Philadelphia, PA

Although some men can hold that feminine performance does not equate to submissive sexual or romantic positioning, to be courted or dominated by a feminine-of-center man would be to disrupt the rules of hegemony that require femininity to be rejected and subordinated. Further, this dynamic would reinforce a homonegative ideology that positions same gender loving men as so removed from true masculinity that they risk being dominated by the feminine-of-center. Such are the pervasive and interacting natures of hegemony, internalized homonegativity, and femmephobia.

Truth: Considerations must always be made for the necessity of the down low

> It kind of divides itself with race, a little bit, for me. I feel like being DL—the term seems to be one that people of color identify with. I don't hear the conversation of people being DL amongst white people. I've never seen or heard white men use DL or down low. White men just happen to be straight, or straight presenting, and they also have wives and children, and then they also have boyfriends or whoever. So, it seems to almost be two different associations, from what I've seen.
>
> David, 32, Charleston, SC

Although hegemonic masculinity requires hypermasculine performance and a rejection of open same gender loving attraction, it seems that some Black same gender loving men have been able to find the balance between hegemonic expectations and their same gender loving desire through the "down low" (the practice of covertly engaging in same gender sexual and romantic interactions while navigating the world as heterosexual) (Robinson, 2009; Snorton, 2014). What stands fascinating is the evolution of the down low over the years. In 2004, Oprah Winfrey, on her self-titled hit television show, introduced many to the concept of the down low (Snorton, 2014). This introduction quickly created an erroneous media zeitgeist in which down low Black men were pinpointed as the reason for rising rates of HIV/AIDS in the Black community (Bleich & Taylor-Clark, 2005; Millett, Malebranche, Mason, & Spikes, 2006; Robinson, 2009; Wheeler et al., 2009; Wolitski, Jones, Wasserman, & Smith, 2006). Highlighting the down low in such a manner was a harm-filled act that further perpetuated overt homonegativity in various sections of the Black community (i.e., church, family, social groups, etc.). The conceptualization of the down low has however shifted over time. What was once deemed a negative label linked to HIV/AIDS proliferation has, in many Black same gender loving circles, become a label that elicits excitement found in secret sensuality, the teetering between the socially accepted and the taboo, and the facade of physical safety found in hegemonic masculinity (McCune, 2008).

Some Black same gender loving men have approached engagement with down low men as a rite of passage into same gender loving life. Many same gender loving men have made sexual and romantic engagement with down low men a lifestyle and solely pick their sexual and romantic partners from this cohort. Some researchers have positioned the down low as an integral feature for Black same gender loving male survival and note that some men face risk if they were to publicly own their sexual and romantic identities (to this, I wonder if we have allowed ourselves to argue in favor of the down low as a white supremacist balm, instead of taking efforts to abolish the white supremacist structures that call for secret sexual and romantic engagement) (Han, 2015). Literature suggests that men who have a greater racial salience (see themselves as "Black same gender loving men" rather than "same gender loving Black men") will choose to engage in down low sexual and romantic interaction as a form of respect to their racial identity (a consequence of internalized homonegativity which states that Blackness leaves no room for same gender loving identity) (McCune, 2008; Robinson, 2009). Other investigations highlight the down low as a sphere of reclamation, in which some same gender loving Black men may choose to ethically sexually and romantically engage in a manner that was once demonized (many down low men have found liberation in embracing a label that emphasizes their participation in secretive sexual and romantic engagement) (McCune, 2008). For many same gender loving Black men, the down low has become a space in which "no fats, no femmes" constraints can be lifted and Black men can explore sexual and romantic attraction beyond the confines of hegemonic masculinity. Despite the benefits of the down low, this space also presents the opportunity for the increased marginalization and subordination of Black masculinities. The secretive nature of down low engagement can lead Black men, fueled by the cognitive dissonance that arises from acknowledging same gender attraction and possessing internalized homonegativity, to potentially enact physical, emotional, spiritual, and mental violence on other Black same gender loving men (Beam, 2008; Boykin, 2006; Grant, 2020b; Robinson, 2009; Snorton, 2014).

It is not the purpose of this chapter to chastise men for identifying with down low culture or wanting to engage in down low practices.

However, it is important to understand the connections of the down low to internalized homonegativity and hegemonic masculinity. The down low exists because Black same gender loving men have internalized homonegativity and perceive risk in exploring their same gender sexual and romantic attractions publicly. Such engagement would contrast social expectations of masculinity and lead to the anticipated consequences of decreased social ranking (i.e., familial and communal ostracization, increased shame, etc.).

What's your truth?

- What are your thoughts and feelings about the down low? What has influenced these thoughts and feelings?
- What factors do you think place Black men as the focus of down low culture?

10 Endured Presence and Homopositivity

**Truth: Although white supremacy distorted Black
sexuality, it could not disrupt the prevailing presence
of same gender loving leadership and expression**

Whiteness has contributed to the distortion, erasure, suppression, and regulation of Black traditions, Black cultures, and Black practices; particularly that of diverse sexual existence and expression. It is however interesting to note that despite the impact of white oppression, Black same gender loving people have resisted, persisted, and continue to thrive in leadership roles throughout the Black community. The Harlem Renaissance, although impacted by social efforts to adhere to respectability, was tapestried with the presence of Black fairies (Black same gender loving men who often presented in women's clothing); it was saturated with Black same gender loving men who possessed presence in conservative media spheres due to their elaborate fraternal support systems, tendencies to marry the opposite sex (which fulfilled social duties), and propensities to financially and sexually interact with white fetishists in ways that depicted liberation and heightened social standing; it was also an era in which art and culture would not have been present without the Niggeratti Society (a historic group of artists and intellectuals during the Harlem Renaissance, many of which were noted to be same gender loving), the solo publication of *FIRE!!!*, and the contribution of same gender loving artists such as Alan Locke, Countee Cullen, Richard Bruce Nugent, Langston Hughes, and Claude McKay (Murray, Roscoe, & Epprecht, 2021; Schwarz, 2003; Thurman et al., 1926).

Extending beyond the timeline of the Harlem Renaissance, advancements in science, agriculture, and Black collegiate education would look different were it not for the contributions of George Washington Carver (Benson, 2018). Music throughout the ages would

DOI: 10.4324/9781003180937-11

not be as developed without the influences of Ma Rainey, Bessie Smith, and Sylvester. Discussions of race, civil rights, and equality for all Black folx would not be as nuanced without the contributions and organizational prowess of figures such as James Baldwin, Bayard Rustin, and James Beam (Baldwin, 1952; Beam, 2008; Rustin, Carbado, & Weise, 2015). Not only is the presence of same gender loving folx inherent to African culture; the presence and influence of same gender loving Black folx are ingredients that have shaped and led Black culture. Many in the Black community, however, have allowed white supremacy to incorrectly assert that homonegativity and same gender loving suppression and regulation are necessary for the maintenance of values that will ensure the survival of Black people. Current events of racial unrest and the senseless killing of Black people by the hands of white supremacists unveil this logic as flawed (Barbot, 2020; Chughtai, 2012). Black adherence to white supremacy will never ensure Black freedom and survival. It is therefore time to rethink the ways the Black community engages sexual diversity. It is time to highlight new narratives and embrace new truths.

> I didn't understand what I was, and I think the older I got, understanding the history of homosexuality and Black people makes me feel a little bit more prideful for being a Black gay male existing in America.
>
> Rammy, 30, Wilson, NC

What's your truth?

- What is your knowledge of same gender loving Black influence on Black culture?
- How does this knowledge shape your beliefs about Black same gender loving people?
- What truths about Black same gender loving folx do you think need to be disseminated?

Truth: The narrative of homonegativity in the Black community often overshadows the homopositivity present throughout generations

Research and literature have often positioned same gender loving Black men solely as victims of oppression. This trend has become so well-known that the Black community has been presumed to be more homonegative than other races (a laughable argument when one realizes that homonegativity is not inherent to Black culture). The truth stands, however, that many Black same gender loving men, across age groups, experience homopositivity in their various communities. Some Black men identified their parents, guardians, and other family members as supports and co-conspirators in protecting them from a homonegative world (Grant, 2020b); other Black same gender loving men recognize religious spaces as positive spheres for both racial and sexual identity development (Grant, 2020b); and others note being exposed to same gender loving individuals in their communities who were well-respected leaders (Grant, 2020b). For some reason, these narratives rarely counterbalance tales of Black homonegativity, which perpetuates a helpless and hopeless picture of Black same gender loving male experiences.

Many of the narratives disseminated about Black same gender loving male life have often come from individuals working within white supremacist institutions (i.e., academia, healthcare, the judiciary system). It is therefore in the best interest of these disseminators—who wish to maintain systems of white supremacy under the guise of educational advancement—to continue the perpetuation of Black same gender loving male trauma narratives. True educational transformation and community impact will occur when Black same gender loving men are afforded the opportunity to distribute their own narratives through multiple mediums. Such methods may challenge the overwhelming narrative of homonegativity within Black life and bring nuance to understandings of same gender loving Black male experiences.

> I came out to my parents in 2018 and my dad's been accepting since day one. Despite him being away for most of my childhood, he still wanted to build a bond. Once I got to college, I strayed from what my family was telling me about my father and started to get to know him, which led to me telling him about my sexuality before anyone in my family. And he was just proud that I had the courage to let him know. Even to this day, I'm very open with him about who I date and he's very open to listening; and that's all I could realty ask for in a parent.
>
> Devin, 25, Charleston, SC

> My pastor, I told him I was gay. He never treated me no kind of way. I was never sat down, ever! He could've sat me down. And to this day I love him like crazy. People in my home church would talk but it wasn't to the point where it affected me.
>
> Avery, 33, Washington, D.C.

I've been warmly welcomed by my fraternity, as well as my chapter. The acceptance and love they have for their members, regardless of their identity, is what drew me to the organization.

Edgar, 30, Lawnside, NJ

My sister was phenomenal. I remember crying to her—she was the first person I came out to. She handled it so well. The freedom she gave that allowed me to be my authentic self and to let go of that baggage I was carrying until I was 26 was amazing.

MJ, 30, Charlotte, NC

Truth: On resilience and Black same gender loving men

Resilience (re·sil·ience /rə'zilyəns/n): the capacity to recover quickly from difficulties; toughness.

Black people are resilient people—such is the narrative many Black folx have embraced with pride. The Black community has endured colonialism, enslavement, Jim Crow, post-racial colorblindness, police brutality, and centuries of other oppressions (Collins, 2004). More narrowly, Black same gender loving men have exhibited resilience through their ability to thrive despite degradation, regulation, ostracization, poverty, homelessness, religious stigma, and the burden of HIV/AIDS (Beam, 2008; Boykin & Shange, 2012 Mumford, 2016). Black people—Black same gender loving men—are resilient! However, one must wonder about the consequences that stem from the message of Black resilience.

The highlighting of Black resilience has aided in justifying the enslavement of Black folx (Collins, 2004). Positioning Black people as physically resilient has led to outcomes such as the exploitation of Saartje/ Saartjie "Sarah" Bartman and the advancement of gynecology and other sciences (Holland, 2017; Parkinson, 2016). The emphasis of Black resilience has, in part, aided in the propagation of post-racial dialogue; similarly, the emphasis of Black same gender loving male resilience has helped incite the dismissal of Black same gender loving male oppression, and has helped promote ideas such as Black same gender loving male privilege (Fitz, 2015; Jones, 2015). While Black resilience highlights the ability of Black folx to overcome challenges, it does little to address or disrupt the systems that have created said challenges. The pressure to remain resilient in the face of oppression has left many Black folx—Black same gender loving men—fatigued. Black same gender loving men need more than resilience. Albeit naïve to demand the immediate dismantling of homonegativity, hegemonic masculinity, and femmephobia, it is recognized that Black same gender loving men would benefit from a framework that facilitates engagement with, rather than the overcoming of, internalized homonegativity. It is my hope that in the next chapter, Black same gender loving men will find the means to exchange resilience for understanding, toughness for truth and vulnerability, and survival for thriving through value-based living.

What's your truth?

- What do you think are the pros and cons of Black resilience (if any)?

11 A Model for Navigating Homonegative Spaces

To this point, numerous truths related to internalized homonegativity and Black same gender loving male experiences have been presented. Some may believe that uncovering truths about internalized homonegativity will lead to overcoming internalized homonegativity. I hope to avoid offering this book as a tool to overcome internalized homonegativity, as minority stress theory highlights that overcoming internalized homonegativity (however that is achieved) will not prevent Black same gender loving men from experiencing the negative mental, emotional, and physical health outcomes that stem from existing in a racist and homonegative society (Barnes & Meyer, 2012; Frost, Levahot, & Meyer, 2015; Grant, 2020b; Meyer, 1995, 2003, 2015; O'Donnell, Meyer, & Schwartz, 2011). As stated in the previous chapter, it is my hope that this text helps readers intentionally engage internalized homonegativity in a way that transcends resilience and facilitates values-driven navigation despite the existence of marginalization and oppression.

Extant models of sexual identity development communicate a narrative in which internalized homonegativity can be overcome, or significantly reduced, with immersion into same gender loving communities and the acquisition of a partner. Vivienne Cass (1979) proposes that people develop homosexual identity as they transition through six distinct stages. The first of these stages is *identity confusion*, in which an individual experiences distress when they identify their behaviors, thoughts, and emotions with homosexuality (Cass, 1984). A person will then experience *identity comparison*, in which they increasingly recognize that their sexual identities differ from those who may identify as heterosexual. The level of distress experienced in this developmental stage is noted to be variable and dependent on the amount of negative appraisal the individual has toward same gender loving identities. After identity comparison, an individual will begin to

DOI: 10.4324/9781003180937-12

develop *identity tolerance,* which Cass (1984) describes as a stage in which a same gender loving person will begin to seek out other same gender loving people for social, emotional, and sexual fulfillment. Cass (1984) highlights that upon engaging with other same gender loving people, a same gender loving individual will achieve *identity acceptance* by immersing themselves in gay culture and adopting a more positive general view of homosexuality (Cass, 1984). After this process, Cass (1984) suggests that an individual will experience a season of *identity pride,* in which they align with same gender loving communities and reject any associations with heterosexuality. Cass (1984) finalizes her model with the *identity synthesis* stage, in which the same gender loving person finds a balance between heterosexual and homosexual alignment without experiencing dissonance or distress related to social group loyalty. While Cass (1984) created a theory of sexual identity actualization that has been used to conceptualize the journeys of many same gender loving people, her model does not generalize to many Black same gender loving male experiences. Many Black same gender loving men may actualize and affirm their identities without experiencing distress about being same gender loving, without joining same gender loving culture, without adopting a same gender loving identity, or without rejecting heterosexuality (Beam, 2008; Boykin & Shange, 2012; Grant, 2020b; Johnson, 2014; Lemelle, 2010; Snorton, 2014). This model of identity development was created from the experiences of white, cisgender, gay and lesbian Australian men and women. It neglects the nuances of the Black same gender loving experience and is blind to the intersections of same gender loving identity development with Black racial, religious, and social identity development (Cass, 1984).

Building upon Cass' stages of development, Coleman (1982) and Troiden (1989a;b) modeled the coming out process in a more condensed manner. According to Coleman (1982), sexual identity development encompasses *pre-coming out,* which occurs when an individual experiences same sex interests, yet has dismissed these notions and have separated themselves from homosexual affiliation. The individual will then explore *coming out* and will disclose their sexual orientation to themselves and others. Coleman (1982) suggests that the same gender loving person will continue to form a same sex attracted identity as they sexually and socially explore with those who possess same sex attractions, pursue and engage in same sex romantic relationships, and integrate themselves into long-term same-sex relationships. Troiden's (1989a;b) stages of identity development have similarly been noted to include *sensitization,* which involves one possessing a feeling of otherness in comparison to the majority heterosexual culture; *identity confusion*, which details dissonant feelings that arise when one acknowledges their experiences of same-sex attraction; *identity assumption*, which occurs when one's sexual identity is accepted and shared with oneself and others; and *identity commitment*, which arises when same gender lovingness is adapted as a way of life, and is evidenced by one's participation in same sex relationships and disclosure of one's identity to both heterosexual and homosexual identifying individuals.

Adding to these stages of coming out, D'Augelli (1995) presents queer identity development as a lifespan process that caters to the fluidity of sexuality, as well as to the various ways sexuality is shaped by one's biology and environmental interactions. Such theory has suggested that the same gender loving experience can be categorized by six distinct stages: *exiting heterosexuality, developing a personal LGB identity, developing a social LGB identity, becoming an LGB offspring, developing an LGB intimacy status, and entering an LGB community* (which speaks to the numerous subcultures within the LGB community) (D'Augelli, & Patterson, 1995). Noting that there typically exists a stage in homosexual identity development in which an individual actively works to cognitively and behaviorally block their same sex attraction, *exiting heterosexuality* and *developing an individual and social LGB identity* describes a releasing of the defensive strategies one holds against their same sex feelings, an embracing of one's same gender sexual and/or romantic attraction, and a disclosing of this attraction to oneself and others. D'Augelli (1995) highlights that *becoming an LGB offspring* occurs when an individual can disclose their sexual identity with their parents or guardians. D'Augelli (1995) also positions *developing an LGB intimacy status* and *entering an LGB community* as behaviors that include engaging in same gender intimate partnerships and participating in social identity disclosures by becoming involved in public LGB+ affairs (D'Augelli & Patterson, 1995). While Coleman (1982), Troiden (1989a;b), and D'Augelli (1995) created more succinct models of sexual identity development, their proposed models are limited by the assertion that identity actualization occurs when one has engaged in relationship formation and identity disclosure. Such achievements have been noted to contrast the priorities of same gender loving Black men, and ignore the intersectional factors that position disclosure and public relationship formation as potential hindrances of Black same gender loving male identity development (Beam, 2008; Fassinger & McCarn, 1996; Grant, 2020b; Johnson, 2014; McCune, 2008; Stone & Ward, 2011).

Possibly the most racially and ethnically considerate of queer identity development models is Morales' (1989) model, which highlights that ethnic queer people reach a state of adaptive functioning when the tensions stemming from allegiance to their racial and sexual selves become reconciled. Morales posits that sexual identity development formation for ethnic folx includes the following stages:

1 **Denial of Conflicts:** The same gender loving person tends to minimize the validity and reality of discrimination they experience as an ethnic person and believe they are treated the same as others. Their sexual orientation may or may not be defined, but they feel their personal lifestyle and sexual preferences have limited consequences in their life.

2 **Bisexual versus Gay/Lesbian:** The preference for some ethnic gays and lesbians is to identify themselves as bisexual rather than gay or lesbian.

3 **Conflicts in Allegiances:** The simultaneous awareness of being the member of an ethnic minority, as well as being gay or lesbian, presents anxiety around the need for these lifestyles to remain separate. Anxiety about betraying either the ethnic minority or the gay/lesbian communities, when preference is given to one over the other, becomes a major concern.

4 **Establishing Priorities in Allegiance:** A primary identification with the ethnic community prevails in this state, and feelings of resentment concerning the lack of integration among the communities becomes a central issue. There are feelings of anger and rage stemming from [the same gender loving person's] experiences of rejection by the gay community because of their ethnicity.

5 **Integrating the Various Communities:** As a [same gender loving] person of color, the need to integrate their lifestyle and develop a multicultural perspective becomes a major concern. Adjusting to the reality of the limited options currently available for [same gender loving] people of color becomes a source of anxiety, facilitating feelings of isolation and alienation.

(Morales, 1989)

Morales' model suggests that some Black same gender loving men may be less advanced in their identity development because they abandon, modify, or repress the development of their sexual selves in order to adhere to the racialized gendered expectations of their racial group (i.e., they remain stuck at stage 3). Morales' (1989) model is often corroborated by discussions of men identifying as "same gender loving Black men" versus "Black same gender loving men." Data suggests that Black men who identify more with their racial identities are often associated with seeking to fulfill the roles of Black masculinity, which leads to outcomes such as perpetuating down low culture, or being less forthcoming with their sexual and romantic orientations in various spaces (Hunter, 2010). Contrastingly, literature suggests that Black men who see their sexual orientations as the more salient identity may engage in practices such as immersing themselves in gay/SGL/queer culture (replicative of Cass' model) and seeking sexual and romantic partnership with white men (a practice that seemingly positions white men, and partnership with white men, as the epitome of gay identity fulfillment) (Hunter, 2010). However, while Morales' (1989) model of sexual identity development makes space for the consideration of diverse racial and ethnic experiences, his conceptualization may not be relevant for some Black same gender loving men. Black men have historically possessed high racial salience and have been reluctant to ignore the prejudices enacted by majority culture (Beam, 2008; Grant, 2020b; Griffin, 2010; Rustin, Carbado, & Weise, 2015; Snorton, 2014). Morales' (1989) conflict of allegiance assertion presents sexual and racial identities as conflicting identities that incite internalized homonegativity, rather than inter-sectional identities that collaboratively inform the overall experience of internalized homonegativity among Black same gender loving men (Crenshaw, 1989).

There exist folx—Black same gender loving men—who hold tensions and homonegative stances as their sexual and romantic attractions in-teract with their race, class, educational rank, socioeconomic status, social caste, and other factors. To suggest that men in these positions are limited in their ability to integrate their identities, or assert that they must immerse themselves into same gender loving culture, find long term partnership, or reconcile their intersectional tensions is anti-therapeutic, potentially detrimental, does not assist same gender loving men in ad-dressing internalized homonegativity, and may contribute to a decreased quality of life. Modeling same gender loving identity through the stan-dards shaped by white liberation produces the same outcomes as per-forming gender through a Eurocentric lens—outcomes that do not benefit Black folx.

Instead of offering a model for sexual identity development, I offer the IONIC model—a framework of therapeutically informed steps that may increase Black same gender loving male understanding of homonegativity in their lives, and assist them in traversing life in a way that most aligns with their values. To live in a homonegative society is to inherit homonegativity. I do not believe that sexual identity, or the reduction of homonegativity, can be developed in stages or phases. I also reject the notion that nuances of sexual identity among all Black same gender loving men can be captured by a single model. I believe one's sexual and romantic identities, identity expressions and endorsed homonegativities exist on a continuum. A same gender loving Black man can be sexually and romantically expressive in one space and conservative in another, without being inherently burdened by internalized homonegativity (to suggest inability of this nuance feels like a white supremacist limitation on the expansive nature of Black navigation). The proposed IONIC model acknowledges and honors that Black same gender loving men have the right and ability to autonomously engage in homonegative spaces, or with homonegative people, as they wish; and asserts that this interaction does not have to lead to the internalization of said homonegativity.

> It wasn't until recently that I realized, my God, look at all the years I've wasted, blaming everyone for this and that. It's time for me to get it together, so that I can be fruitful and enjoy my life, and people can experience the me without brokenness or shame.
>
> Marcus, 35, Clifton, MD

> It wasn't until recently that I've accepted myself and I think now it's a matter of navigating life and figuring out how to walk again—how to navigate this world. I want to feel more fulfilled.
>
> Rammy, 30, Wilson, NC

The IONIC model: Introduction and rationale

The foundation of the IONIC model is inspired by Marsha Linehan's (2017) radical acceptance, found in dialectical behavior therapy (DBT). This ideology suggests that individuals cannot change invalidating environments, nor the thoughts and emotions that arise from interacting with invalidating environments; to attempt such an endeavor would reinforce suffering. The IONIC model is also informed by the tenets of self-compassion, championed by Kristen Neff, which advocates for self-kindness rather than self-judgment, the sharing of human experience over isolation, and exhibiting non-judgment to the present moment rather than overidentifying with present events (Germer & Neff, 2013). Psychologically inclined individuals may assume that the best treatment for individuals living with internalized homonegativity may be to reduce or avoid their experiences of external and internal homonegativity. The extant literature on therapeutic treatment for lesbian, gay, bisexual, and other non-heterosexual (LGB+) individuals often focuses on coming out and affirming one in developing a public identity (Coleman & Dunn, 1996; das Nair & Butler 2012; Safren & Rogers, 2001). However, treatments for disorders such as anxiety and depression communicate how understanding and managing adverse experiences, through exposure, often reduce the distress affiliated with said experiences (Arch & Craske, 2008; Pachankis, Hatzenbuehler, Rendina, Safren, & Parsons, 2015). Therefore, some Black same gender loving men may benefit from interacting with internal and external homonegativity as a way to uncover personal truths and engage behaviors most aligned with their values. By presenting the steps of the IONIC model, with therapeutic justifications and examples of the model's application, it is my hope that Black same gender loving men will be able to effectively confront and navigate internal and external homonegative experiences.

Consideration: Why stay in an environment that does not accept all your identities?

Why would anyone continue to exist in spaces—familial, religious, or social—that do not accept and affirm their identities? For that, I am unsure. There exist courageous same gender loving Black men who refuse to participate in spaces that do not affirm their same gender loving identities. There also exist equally courageous Black same gender loving men who are drawn, due to their values or commitment to various spaces and people, to navigate environments in which their identities are not be accepted and affirmed. While therapeutic treatment often advocates for same gender loving people to come out and solely exist in affirming spaces, this goal may not be congruent with the values of Black same gender loving men—values centered on community engagement, familial connection, and spiritual involvement.

Situation: The case of Jamil

It has been three years since Jamil has moved away from his hometown, Mobile, AL, to Seattle, WA for work. During this time, Jamil has acknowledged and affirmed his identity as a Black same gender loving man. In celebration of his new employment, Jamil's older brother decided surprise him with an unexpected visit. The two have always been close, so Jamil was excited to receive his brother.

However, Jamil has never disclosed his same gender loving identity to his family. On the third day of his brother's visit, a commercial for the hit show *Pose* appeared while the two were watching television. Jamil was struck as his brother scoffed at the television and exclaimed, "I can't believe they're showing that gay shit on TV."

The IONIC model: Application

Identify
Observe
Notice
Integrate
Choose

The first two actions of the IONIC model encourage Black same gender loving men to *observe and describe*. These mindfulness-based skills are clinically supported to assist same gender loving Black men in approaching homonegative environments and experiences with objectivity (Linehan, 2017; Neff, 2003). They also promote an environmental awareness and engagement that reduces the risk of cognitively or emotionally overidentifying with the homonegative event (Harris & Hayes, 2019; Linehan, 2017; Neff, 2003). Successfully observing an experience, and describing said experience, shows the engager that they do not have to "become the event." The experience of homonegativity does not have to lead to the development and maintenance of internalized homonegativity, as frequently posited by research. The objective awareness of a homonegative occurrence can assist Black same gender loving men in separating themselves from the event they are navigating, which may provide a buffer against the internalization of homonegativity.

1   **IDENTIFY** what is happening in the situation.

This step draws from DBT's checking the facts, which can aid in grounding and emotion regulation. Before falling into a hyper-focusing of the homonegative experience, objectively figure out what is going on. You may want to ask yourself:

- Where am I?
- What did I just experience?
- What did I see?
- What did I hear?

- Who are the people involved in the experience?
- What was just communicated?

2   **OBSERVE** what is going on internally and externally.

As you are collecting data about the situation and your external environment, it may be helpful to be mindful of your cooccurring internal processes.

- How is my body responding to this moment (breathing, sweating, heart rate, etc.)?
- What am I thinking?

In the case of Jamil

Jamil identifies that he and his brother were watching television and a commercial for *Pose* appeared. Jamil then heard his brother say, "I can't believe they're showing that gay shit on TV."

Jamil may observe that he is feeling unsafe; his heart may be pounding and he may be sweating. He may endorse worries that he will be rejected by his brother if he discloses his identity. Jamail may notice feelings of anger toward his brother's remark, as evidenced by an internal flush of heat or an inability to focus his thoughts in the moment. On the other hand, Jamil may feel safe, as he knows his brother to be "someone who says whatever comes to his mind."

The next step of the IONIC model is rooted in cognitive behavioral therapy's cognitive restructuring (i.e., being open to, and practicing, new and alternative forms of thinking) and experiential exposure (i.e., allowing oneself to engage in a distressing situation that is usually avoided or manipulated to reduce feelings of distress) (Acarturk, Cuijpers, van Straten, & de Graaf, 2009). Previous chapters have discussed how white supremacy has conditioned same gender loving men to endorse the cognitive distortion of black and white thinking—thinking that reinforces the binary of heterosexuality as "normal" and "good" and same gender loving identity as "abnormal" and "bad." Previous sections have also noted that Black same gender loving men, fueled by internalized homonegativity, often find themselves isolating from homonegative environments (or environments they perceive to be homonegative) in order to regulate the distress experienced from external and internal homonegativity. Immersion in, and assessment of, homonegative engagements invite experiential exposure, which may prompt a cognitive restructuring that disrupts binary adherence. Same gender loving Black men who immerse themselves in homonegative experiences may begin to scrutinize the oppressive systems that maintain hegemonic masculinity through sexuality- and gender-based binaries (this examination can be executed through experience and does not require a specific level of knowledge or education); they will begin to understand their responsive thoughts and feelings and weigh whether these reactions positively impact their well-being and self-appraisals; they will start to weigh the short- and long-term impacts of engaging in homonegative environments; and they will begin to explore their options for present and future engagement.

3   **NOTICE** the oppressive systems and factors that inform this moment. Notice the parts of yourself you're being encouraged to relinquish, or the patterns you're being encouraged to participate in during this situation. You may want to ask yourself:

- Am I on the verge of being outed?
- Am I feeling secondary shame from someone or something else being the target of homonegativity?
- Is my environment calling me to participate in homonegative thoughts or actions?
- Is the homonegativity I'm experiencing originating from a space I previously perceived to be safe (i.e., familial, platonic, romantic)?
- How is my dignity, integrity, or sense of self being challenged in this moment?
- What are the perceived institutions or systems facilitating this challenge?

Note: While immersing oneself within, and examining, a homonegative experience may seem difficult, practicing this step when alone is valuable and may increase mastery of improving objective awareness of thoughts, feelings, and intentions.

In the case of Jamil

While Jamil is unable to quote gender and sexuality scholars, he may notice that he comes from a southern family who proudly asserts their traditional values. Jamil may acknowledge his family's expectations on what it means to be a strong Black man. Jamil may also identify that he and his brothers have been indoctrinated in traditionally masculine spaces that normalize gay bashing. From this, Jamil may develop context for his brother's remark while remaining objective to the situation.

As one progresses through the IONIC model, one is prompted to place less emphasis on the present situation and focus on oneself as the only constant throughout one's life experiences. My work with same gender loving men has revealed that this cohort often experiences victimization from numerous sources. Using the IONIC model to approach homonegative people and situations objectively allows same gender loving men to conceptualize themselves as independent beings with the power to navigate as they wish.

The fourth step of the IONIC model is inspired by the concept of choice point in Acceptance and Commitment Therapy, which states that every situation, thought, emotion, physiological response, and behavior can lead us toward, and away from, our value systems (Harris & Hayes, 2019). This concept may seem simple, however things become more complex when conflicting values arise in a single situation. Some same gender loving Black men may choose to move away from their value of peace and comfort in one space, to move toward their value of maintaining relationship with loved ones who perpetuate homonegativity. Other Black same gender loving men may opt to move away from their value of pleasing loved ones, to adhere to their value of opposing homonegativity. At its core, this step calls for objective understanding of one's environment, one's mental and emotional states, the cultural and systemic dynamics and expectations of the moment, and one's values. Further, this step recognizes that we all have varying capacities to endure discomfort and violence depending on who and what we value in a given space.

4　**INTEGRATE** the previously collected pieces of information (from Steps 1-3) and assess what thoughts, emotions, and behaviors align most with your value system. You may want to ask yourself:

- What do I want to achieve at this moment?
- Do I want to stand out as a same gender loving individual?
- Do I prioritize "going with the flow" of my environment?
- Am I ready to combat the homonegative thinking of my social group?
- Do I share some of the homonegative ideologies expressed by my group?

How can I identify my values?

This is a question I'm often asked in therapeutic practice. Many clinicians use the Acceptance and Commitment Therapy (ACT) values card sort activity to assist clients in understanding their values toward self, family, and other facets of life (Harris & Hayes, 2019). I, however, find the following task to be more impactful and experiential when it comes to exploring one's values in relation to sexual and romantic attraction and identity:

> Think of a time when you experienced a hurtful event around your identity. It could have been a time when you didn't think of yourself as same gender loving; it could have been a time when you acknowledged your identity but were uncomfortable with disclosure. In that event, what did you need to make the experience less distressing? Dig deep and keep repeating the question—"what did I need?"—until you've run out of possible answers. Then ask yourself, "Which of my past needs do I desire currently?" That consistency of need communicates what you value. It could be protection, honesty, or the presence of someone who loves you unconditionally. Noticing this, how can you honor your values and give yourself what you need at any given moment?

In the case of Jamil

Despite understanding his familial background and upbringing, Jamil may simultaneously acknowledge the work he has undergone to affirm his identity over three years. He may remember the times in the past where he remained silent in the face of homonegativity. He may perceive his anger as a righteous anger that aligns with his value of desiring to be in spaces that affirm same gender loving folx. Jamil's fear may indicate a value of wanting to preserve the bond between he and his brother. His racing thoughts may indicate the presence of multiple, possibly conflicting, values arising in the moment.

5 **CHOOSE** how you'll participate in the present situation and how you'll affirm yourself.

I once had a patient describe life as a "choose your adventure game," in which every decision they made led to consequences. They could not have been more profound in this assessment. However, one cannot fully experience the outcome of an event if one does not actively participate in the event. While we cannot control our environments and the actions of those around us, we have control over how we receive and respond to our surroundings. By this logic, the narrative of Black same gender loving men having no power to combat, or reinforce, homonegative environments is fallacy ridden. By integrating internal and external data, and understanding their values, Black same gender loving men can affirm themselves and fully interact with their environments (regardless of whether they opposed or reinforced homonegativity). Feel free to reread that last sentence, because it gives Black same gender loving men permission to radically accept and compassionately understand their present relationship with homonegativity.

Research often identifies affirmation of sexual orientation, and performed outness, as the only ways same gender loving folx can experience reduced distress related to their identities. I, however, identify sexual orientation as part of the entire being and suggest that affirmation of the whole self is what will reduce distress. I also recognize that one can be internally affirmed in an externally unfirming environment, and still choose to engage with said environment. It is through this understanding that Black same gender loving men will be able to objectively identify and accept the internal and external tensions that arise in homonegative spaces—understanding that they are not responsible for these tensions—and fully participate with their environment in a value-driven manner, without sacrificing or damaging their sense of self. Social tensions and stigmas, prejudices, sufferings, and systemic oppression are a part of the human experience—white supremacy has made it so, is responsible for shifting this dynamic, and has presently refused to change the status quo (Germer & Neff, 2013). Despite these trials, there exists freedom in nonjudgmentally living a life centered upon values and the awareness that values can change as one's environment changes (Germer & Neff, 2013). There is no right or single way to be same gender loving in any given space. The most effective way is to understand one's internal and external truths and fully participate in one's life based on these truths.

In the case of Jamil

For Jamil, full participation with the moment could present in various ways. Jamil, personally affirmed in his identity, may choose to ignore his brother's ignorance and mindfully focus on watching television. Jamil could choose to pause the television and disclose his identity to his brother. He could also engage in challenging his brother's homonegative remark and educating his brother on why such remarks are violent. Whatever Jamil decides, his full participation with homonegativity does not have to lead to the diminishing of his identity or the endorsing of beliefs that present his identity as flawed, subordinate, or abnormal.

What's your truth?

Take a minute to think about the IONIC model.

*   Where and how could you use this framework?
*   What are some of your perceived challenges or barriers regarding the model?
*   What are some factors that may aid you in successfully following the model?

As you implement this model in your lives through personal application and/or clinical work, it may be beneficial to record situations that call for the IONIC model's use and track the ways in which the model can be utilized over time.

Epilogue

A truth on community

Surveying the research, literature, and qualitative accounts of homo-negativity among Black same gender loving men highlights one ulti-mate truth—homonegativity significantly oppresses same gender loving Black men by leveraging their desire for community against their need for sexual and romantic identity acceptance and affirmation. While curating this work, I invited my study participants to close their interviews by identifying what Black same gender loving men experi-encing internalized homonegativity need in order to thrive while living in systemically oppressive environments. To date, all responses have highlighted community as a tool to help Black same gender loving men understand their identities, sit with internalized homonegativity, and navigate life in a manner most aligned with their values.

To honor this theme, I end the present work by sharing my re-spondents' takes on the ways community has positively impacted their lives:

> My friends—when I was finally able to release all that guilt and shame and be honest—I feel like a lot of Black same sex men hide behind a shield of who they want to be. Being able to take that off and be your authentic self with friends has been a positive for sure!
>
> MJ, 30, Charlotte, NC

> When you grow up, in many ways you feel isolated cast off, othered; although in the back of your mind you know there has to be other people out there who feel that way. I think growing up and eventually coming into community, and finding other folx who've had similar experiences, and learning about folx who've

traversed this terrain; that's the liberation part. It's almost a collective resistance, empowerment through resistance.

Simeon, 31, Brooklyn NY

That sense of community. I've gotten exposure to many people who've helped me be comfortable, identify with, and relate to others who love someone of the same sex. I don't like to identify as masculine or feminine but being exposed to community has helped me be comfortable with both forms.

Justin, 30, Cleveland, OH

I came out to my best friend after freshman year in college, during the summertime when we were all back home. I remember I was on my way home and my alternator had gone out by a gas station down the road. So, I was waiting for my mom to come and my best friend of course had joined me. So, my mom comes and hadn't seen him in several months, so they were catching up. I hear out the side of my ear, they're having a conversation about dating. And she asks him, "Do you have any girlfriends?" And he says, "No not really. There are girls I just talk to." And they laugh and giggle and my mom goes, "Yeah, you know because there are guys out here dating guys so I didn't know if you were a part of that clan too!" My best friend is very intuitive and when she said that I was faced toward the car, but he could see that I was irritated. He didn't say anything in that moment, but when I get home, my best friend calls me and says, "Did you make it home? There's something I need to ask you." And I already knew what it was. But he was like, "Before I ask you, I want you to know that I love you for who you are. I had an experience this year where a guy in my dorm was gay. A lot of guys, including myself, made fun of him and it hurt him so much that he dropped out of school." And it was that moment that taught him that he never wanted to be that type of influence on anyone else. So, he asked me, "Are you gay?" And I felt like that was the moment I was waiting for, that I didn't know I needed at that time. And I said, "Yes." And he said, "Okay, I need you to know I'm always going to be your best friend and I'm always going to love you." That night we talked until almost 4am. At the time, I think it was my first time also talking to a guy and I was super excited I could share that with my best friend and not be shunned for it; it felt so good! Coming out to him led me to come out to my brother, then my peers, and then my mom and grandparents.

Rammy, 30, Wilson, NC

Conducting this work has highlighted that internalized homo-negativity among Black same gender loving men is a chameleon-eqsue phenomenon that engages and impacts Black same gender loving men differently. The experience of internalized homonegativity across same gender loving Black men emphasizes the consequence of Black folx's conditioning in a white supremacist society. This conditioning has attempted to erase the queerness that is common to the Black experience; it has rooted Black manhood in a caricatured performance measured by, and against, white masculinity; and it has sought to convince Black same gender loving men to align their values of gender, sexuality, and privilege with structures that reinforce their subordination and marginalization. I hope this work helps Black same gender loving men become increasingly aware of the systems that thrive on their oppression and aid this cohort in opposing those systems through value-based living. It is not the responsibility of Black same gender loving men to overcome homonegativity or make society less homonegative. The responsibility of dismantling systems of oppression should fall on those who have constructed, and continue to benefit from, these systems. However, Black same gender loving men do not have to remain victims of homonegativity. They deserve to thrive in a homonegative world by radically using their thoughts, emotions, and behaviors to live in congruence with their values.

Family members and friends of Black same gender loving men, wishing to affirm or maintain relationships with their loved ones, often inquire how they can affirm Black same gender loving men. The men I have interviewed frequently emphasize the importance of "love" from their family members and friends (Grant, 2020b). I however wonder how these men conceptualize love. For those whose communities originate in collectivism (i.e., the Black community), love could mean acts of public respect, provision, unwavering presence, or communal recognition and status. Future research would benefit from further investigating the ways Black same gender loving men conceptualize the love they desire from their communities.

Some clinicians, advocates, and healers additionally seek to discover how they can affirm Black same gender loving male identities. My work has revealed that no two Black same gender loving men are the same. There therefore exists no general prescription or recommendation on how to address Black same gender loving male needs. Individually, clinicians, providers, and advocates would benefit from confronting their positive and negative biases toward Black same gender loving men and understanding how these biases inform the ways they professionally engage Black same gender loving men and their issues. While there exists harm in not affirming Black same gender loving male identities, there is also risked harm in assuming that the issues faced by Black same gender loving men are rooted in their racial, sexual, or romantic identities. I encourage professionals working with this cohort on individual, communal, and systemic levels to use tools, such as hermeneutic qualitative research, to fully understand the issues most relevant to this cohort at any given time.

Although the present work has provided a foundation for understanding internalized homonegativity among Black same gender loving men, there is a breadth of knowledge that has not been discovered. The men in this work present experiences from specific socioeconomic, ethnic, educational, ability-based, and other backgrounds. The richness of their lives and perspectives were only partially captured in the text. Future research is needed in order to expand not only the present voices, but the narratives of men who differ demographically. The work in understanding internalized homonegativity and the lived experiences of Black same gender loving men is far from complete. This text serves as an introduction to a phenomenon that deserves increased exploration regarding its past, present, and future contexts.

References

Acarturk, C., Cuijpers, P., van Straten, A., & de Graaf, R. (2009). Psychological treatment of social anxiety disorder: A meta-analysis. *Psychological Medicine, 39*, 241–254.

Alexander, M. (2010; 2012). *The new jim crow: Mass incarceration in the age of colorblindness.* New Press.

Alexander, W. H. (2004). Homosexual and racial identity conflicts and depression among African-American gay males. *Trotter Review, 16*(1), 71–103.

Allen, Q. (2016). 'Tell your own story': Manhood, masculinity and racial socialization among black fathers and their sons. *Ethnic and Racial Studies, 39*(10), 1831–1848. doi: 10.1080/01419870.2015.1110608

Amola, O., & Grimmett, M. A. (2015). Sexual identity, mental health, HIV risk behaviors, and internalized homophobia among Black men who have sex with men. *Journal of Counseling & Development, 93*(2), 236–246. doi: 10.1002/j.1556-6676.2015.00199.x

Anderson, E. (2005). Orthodox and inclusive masculinity: Competing masculinities among heterosexual men in a feminized terrain. *Sociological Perspectives, 48*(3), 337–355. doi: 10.1525/sop.2005.48.3.337

Anti-Defamation League (n.d.). Gender-neutral pronouns make headlines. Retrieved from https://www.adl.org/education/resources/tools-and-strategies/gender-neutral-pronouns-make-headlines?gclid=CjwKCAiAr6-ABhAfEiwADO4sfV6s6YOyY8U4Wht0Vk2dvOonJM1FxXU55BQ4CR-879lTYVuP7VblMBoC4nsQAvD_BwE

Apple Podcasts (2018–2021). Pour minds podcast. https://podcasts.apple.com/us/podcast/pour-minds-podcast/id1438182646

Arber, W. L., & Sayad, B. W. (2018). *Human sexuality: Diversity in contemporary society.* McGraw-Hill Education.

Arch, J. J., & Craske, M. G. (2008). Acceptance and commitment therapy and cognitive behavioral therapy for anxiety disorders: Different treatments, similar mechanisms? *Clinical Psychology (New York, N.Y.), 15*(4), 263–279. doi: 10.1111/j.1468-2850.2008.00137.x

Arimoro, A. E. (2018). When love is a crime: Is the criminalisation of same sex relations in Nigeria a protection of Nigerian culture? *The Liverpool Law Review*, *39*(3), 221–238. doi: 10.1007/s10991-018-9217-y

Assunção, M. (2020, July 10). Billy Porter on growing up gay in black community: 'It's a very homophobic community across the board'. Retrieved from https://www.nydailynews.com/snyde/ny-billy-porter-eichner-homophobia-transphobia-black-community-20200710-3inlyt2h25cmfpawcvsodvioda-story.html

Awondo, P., Geschiere, P., & Reid, G. (2012). Homophobic Africa? Toward a more nuanced view. *African Studies Review*, *55*(3), 145–168. doi: 10.1017/S0002020600007241

Baldwin, J. (1952). *Go tell it on the mountain*. New York, NY: Dell Publishing.

Balsam, K. F., Molina, Y., Beadnell, B., Simoni, J., & Walters, K. (2011). Measuring multiple minority stress: The LGBT people of color micro-aggressions scale. *Cultural Diversity & Ethnic Minority Psychology*, *17*(2), 163–174. doi: 10.1037/a0023244

Barbot, O. (2020). George Floyd and our collective moral injury. *American Journal of Public Health (1971)*, *110*(9), 1253–1253. doi: 10.2105/AJPH.2020.305850

Barker, C., Pistrang, N., & Elliott, R. (2016). *Research methods in clinical psychology: An introduction for students and practitioners*. New York: Wiley.

Barnes, D. M., & Meyer, I. H. (2012). Religious affiliation, internalized homophobia, and mental health in lesbians, gay men, and bisexuals. *American Journal of Orthopsychiatry*, *82*(4), 505–515. doi: 10.1111/j.1939-0025.2012.01185.x

Barvosa, E. (2014). Unconscious bias in the Suppressive Policing of Black and Latino men and boys: Neuroscience, borderlands theory, and the policy-making quest for just policing. *Politics, Groups, and Identities*, *2*(2), 260–283. https://doi.org/10.1080/21565503.2014.912137

Basaria, S. Dr. (2014). Male hypogonadism. *The Lancet (British Edition)*, *383*(9924), 1250–1263. doi: 10.1016/S0140-6736(13)61126-5

Battle, J., & Bennett, N. (2008). Striving for place: Lesbian, gay, bisexual, and transgender (LGBT) people. In A. Hornsby (Ed.), *A companion to African American history* (pp. 412–438). essay, Blackwell Publishing.

Beachy, R. (2010). The German invention of homosexuality. *The Journal of Modern History*, *82*(4), 801–838. doi: 10.1086/656077

Beam, J. (2008). *In the life: A Black gay anthology*. Washington, DC: RedBone Press.

Beck, A. T., Steer, R. A., & Brown, G. K. (1996). *Manual for the Beck Depression Inventory-II*. San Antonio, TX: Psychological Corporation.

Beck, J. S. (2011). *Cognitive behavior therapy: Basics and beyond* (2nd ed.). Guilford Press.

Beeson, D. (2018, February 08). A brief history of George Washington Carver: The greatest 'bisexual' black scientist of his time. Retrieved from https://www.gaystarnews.com/article/george-washington-carver-facts/

Berg, R. C., Munthe-Kaas, H. M., & Ross, M. W. (2016). Internalized homonegativity: A systematic mapping review of empirical research. *Journal of Homosexuality*, *63*(4), 541–558. doi: 10.1080/00918369.2015. 1083788

Blank, H. (2012). *Straight: The surprisingly short history of heterosexuality.* Beacon Press.

Blay, Z. (2015). 4 'Reverse racism' myths that need to stop. Retrieved from https://www.huffingtonpost.ca/entry/reverse-racism-isnt-a-thing_n_55d60a 91e4b07addcb45da97

Bleich, S., & Taylor-Clark, K. (2005). Black men on the "down-low" and the HIV epidemic: The need for research and intervention strategies. *Harvard Journal of African American Public Policy*, *11*, 13.

Boykin, K. (2006). *Beyond the down low: Sex, lies, and denial in black America.* New York: Carroll & Graf.

Boykin, K., & Shange, N. (2012). *For colored boys who have considered suicide when the rainbow is still not enough: Coming of age, coming out, and coming home* (1st Magnus ed.). Magnus Books.

Buchbinder, D. (2013). *Studying men and masculinities.* Abingdon, UK: Routledge.

Burke, T., & Brown, B. (2021). *You are your best thing: Vulnerability, shame resilience and the Black experience: An anthology.* London: Vermilion.

Butler, A., & Walton, J. (2021). The Black Church. Public Broadcasting Service. Retrieved from https://www.pbs.org/wgbh/americanexperience/ features/godinamerica-black-church/

Butler, J. (1988). Performative acts and gender constitution: An essay in phenomenology and feminist theory. *Theatre Journal*, *40* (4), 519–531

Carrillo, H., & Hoffman, A. (2018). From MSM to heteroflexibilities: Non-exclusive straight male identities and their implications for HIV prevention and health promotion. *Rethinking MSM, Trans* and Other Categories in HIV Prevention*, 105–118. https://doi.org/10.4324/9781315151120-8

Cass, V. C. (1984). Homosexual identity formation: Testing a theoretical model. *The Journal of Sex Research*, *20*(2), 143–167. doi: 10.1080/002244984 09551214

Caswell, M., Migoni, A. A., Geraci, N., & Cifor, M. (2017). 'To be able to imagine otherwise': Community archives and the importance of re-presentation. *Archives and Records (Abingdon, England)*, *38*(1), 5–26. doi: 10.1080/23257962.2016.1260445

Centers for Disease Control & Prevention (2021). HIV and African American People. Retrieved from https://www.cdc.gov/hiv/group/racialethnic/african americans/index.html

Choi, K., Paul, J., Ayala, G., Boylan, R., & Gregorich, S. E. (2013). Experiences of discrimination and their impact on the mental health among African American, Asian and Pacific Islander, and Latino men who have sex with men. *American Journal of Public Health*, *103*(5), 868–874. doi: 10.2105/ AJPH.2012.301052

Chughtai, A. (2021, April 18). Know their names: Black people killed by the police in the US. Retrieved from https://interactive.aljazeera.com/aje/2020/ know-their-names/index.html

Coleman, E. (1982). Developmental stages of the coming-out process. *The American Behavioral Scientist (Beverly Hills)*, *25*(4), 469–482. doi: 10.1177/ 000276482025004009

Coleman, M., & Dunn, P. (1996). Pink therapy: A guide for counsellors and therapists working with lesbian, gay and bisexual clients Dominic Davies and Charles Neal (eds) Open University Press, 1996; £16.99 pbk. *Probation Journal*, *43*(4), 223–224. doi: 10.1177/026455059604300414

Collins, P. H. (2006). *Black sexual politics: African Americans, gender, and the new racism*. Routledge.

Collins, H. P., & Bilge, S. (2021). *Intersectionality*. Polity Press.

Compton, J. (2018, October 28). 'You can't undo surgery': More parents of intersex babies are rejecting operations. Retrieved from https://www.nbcnews. com/feature/nbc-out/you-can-t-undo-surgery-more-parents-intersex-babies-are-n923271

Connell, R. (1987). *Gender and power: Society, the person, and sexual politics*. Stanford, CA: Stanford University Press.

Connell, R. W. (1995). *Masculinities*. Berkeley: University of California Press.

Connell, R. W., & Messerschmidt, J. W. (2005). Hegemonic masculinity: Rethinking the concept. *Gender & Society*, *19*(6), 829–859. doi: 10.1177/ 0891243205278639

Creighton, S. (2001). Surgery for intersex. *Journal of the Royal Society of Medicine*, *94*(5), 218–220. doi: 10.1177/014107680109400505

Crenshaw, K. (1989). Demarginalizing the intersection of race and sex: A Black feminist critique of antidiscrimination doctrine, feminist theory and antiracist politics. *University of Chicago Legal Forum: Vol. 1989*, Article 8.

Crichlow, W. (2004). *Buller men and batty bwoys: Hidden men in Toronto and Halifax Black communities*. Toronto: University of Toronto Press.

Crowell, S. E., Beauchaine, T. P., & Linehan, M. M. (2009). A biosocial developmental model of borderline personality: Elaborating and extending Linehan's theory. *Psychological Bulletin*, *135*(3), 495–510. doi: 10.1037/a0015616

D'Augelli, A. R., Grossman, A. H., & Starks, M. T. (2005). Parents' awareness of lesbian, gay, and bisexual youths' sexual orientation. *Journal of Marriage and Family*, *67*(2), 474–482. doi: 10.1111/j.0022-2445.2005.00129.x

D'Augelli, A. R., & Patterson, C. (1995). *Lesbian, gay, and bisexual identities over the lifespan: Psychological perspectives*. New York: Oxford University Press. doi: 10.1093/acprof:oso/9780195082319.001.0001

Dade, C. (2012). Blacks, gays, and the church: A complex relationship. National Public Radio. Retrieved from https://www.npr.org/2012/05/22/ 153282066/blacks-gays-and-the-church-a-complex-relationship

Dancy, T. E. (2011a). Colleges in the making of manhood and masculinity: Gendered perspectives on African American males. *Gender and Education*, *23*(4), 477–495. https://doi.org/10.1080/09540253.2010.508454

Dancey, T. E. (2011b). Becoming men in burning sands: Student identity, masculinity, and image construction in Black Greek-letter collegiate fraternities. In M. W. Hughey & G. Parks (Eds.), *Black Greek-letter organizations 2.0 New Directions in the study of African American fraternities and sororities* (pp. 95–111). essay, University Press of Mississippi.

Dangerfield II, D. T., Williams, J. E., Bass, A. S., Wynter, T., & Bluthenthal, R. N. (2019). Exploring religiosity and spirituality in the sexual decision-making of black gay and bisexual men. *Journal of Religion and Health, 58*(5), 1792–1802. doi: 10.1007/s10943-019-00845-3

das Nair, R., & Butler, C. (2012). *Intersectionality, sexuality, and psychological therapies: Working with lesbian, gay, and bisexual diversity* (1st ed.). Wiley.

Dean, J. J. (2013). Heterosexual masculinities, anti-homophobias, and shifts in hegemonic masculinity: The identity practices of Black and white heterosexual men. *Sociological Quarterly, 54*(4), 534–560. doi: 10.1111/tsq.12036

DeCarlo, J. (2021). Understanding folx as a linguistic marker of progressive social personae [Unpublished master's thesis]. San Francisco State University.

Delgado, R., Stefancic, J., & Harris, A. P. (2017). *Critical race theory: An introduction* (3rd ed.). New York: New York University Press.

DeSantis, A., & Coleman, M. (2008). Not on my line: Attitudes about homosexuality in Black fraternities. *Black Greek-letter organizations in the twenty-first century.* University Press of Kentucky

Donaghue, C. (2015). *Sex outside the lines: Authentic sexuality in a sexually dysfunctional culture.* BenBella Books, Inc.

Dorahy, M., Corry, M., Shannon, M., Webb, K., McDermott, B., Ryan, M., & Dyer, K. (2012; 2013). Complex trauma and intimate relationships: The impact of shame, guilt and dissociation. *Journal of Affective Disorders, 147*(1), 72–79. doi: 10.1016/j.jad.2012.10.010

Downs, A. (2005). *The velvet rage: What it really means to grow up gay in a straight mans world.* Cambridge, MA: Da Capo Lifelong Books.

Drage, G. (1885). *The Criminal Code of the German Empire.* London: Chapman and Hall.

Dube, S. R., Anda, R. F., Felitti, V. J., Chapman, D. P., Williamson, D. F., & Giles, W. H. (2001). Childhood abuse, household dysfunction, and the risk of attempted suicide throughout the life span: Findings from the adverse childhood experiences study. *JAMA: The Journal of the American Medical Association, 286*(24), 3089–3096. doi: 10.1001/jama.286.24.3089

DuBois, W. E. B. (1903). "The Talented Tenth" in Washington, B.T. *The Negro Problem: A Series of Articles by Representative Negroes of To-day,* essay, J. Pott & Company.

Edwards, W. (2016). Measuring relationship satisfaction: Is it possible for male couples to be satisfied in a relationship? *Deviant Behavior, 37*(8). 931–951. doi: 10.1080/01639625.2016.1156983

Faderman, L. (2016). *The gay revolution: The story of the struggle*. New York: Simon & Schuster *Paperbacks*.

Falk, K. (1923). "Gleichgeschlechtliches Leben bei einigen Negerstamme Angolas" ("Same-Sex Life among a Few Negro Tribes of Angola" (translated by Bradley Rose). *Archiv fir Anthropologie n.s. 20*: 42–45.

Fassinger, R. E., & McCarn, S. R. (1996). Revisioning sexual minority identity formation: A new model of lesbian identity and its implication for counseling and research. *The Counseling Psychologist, 24*(*3*), 508–534. doi: 10.11 77/0011000096243011

Fausto-Sterling, A. (2020). *Sexing the body: Gender politics and the construction of Sexuality*. Basic Books.

Ferber, A. L. (2007). The construction of black masculinity: White supremacy now and then. *Journal of Sport and Social Issues, 31*(1), 11–24. doi: 10.1177/0193723506296829

Fields, E. L., Bogart, L. M., Smith, K. C., Malebranche, D. J., Ellen, J., & Schuster, M. A. (2015). "I always felt I had to prove my manhood": Homosexuality, masculinity, gender role strain, and HIV risk among young black men who have sex with men. *American Journal of Public Health, 105*(1), 122–131. https://doi.org/10.2105/ajph.2013.301866

Fitz, J. (2015). Unmasking Black gay privilege. Retrieved from https://www.huffpost.com/entry/unmasking-black-gay-privilege_b_6978224

Flannigan-Saint-Aubin, A. (1993). "Black gay male" discourse: Reading race and sexuality between the lines. *Journal of the History of Sexuality, 3*(3), 468–490.

Ford, O. (2015). From navigation to negotiation: An examination of the lived experiences of black gay male alumni of historically black colleges and universities. *Journal of Homosexuality, 62*(3), 353–373. doi: 10.1080/009183 69.2014.972814

Foster, M. L., Arnold, E., Rebchook, G., & Kegeles, S. M. (2011). 'It's my inner strength': Spirituality, religion and HIV in the lives of young African American men who have sex with men. *Culture, Health & Sexuality, 13*(9), 1103–1117. doi: 10.1080/13691058.2011.600460

Foucault, M. (2012). *The history of sexuality: An introduction*. Westminster: Knopf Doubleday Publishing Group.

Frost, D. M., Lehavot, K., & Meyer, I. H. (2015). Minority stress and physical health among sexual minority individuals. *Journal of Behavioral Medicine, 38*(1), 1–8. doi: 10.1007/s10865-013-9523-8

Fuller-Thomson, E., Baird, S. L., Dhrodia, R., & Brennenstuhl, S. (2016). The association between adverse childhood experiences (ACEs) and suicide attempts in a population-based study. *Child: Care, Health & Development, 42*(5), 725–734. 10.1111/cch.12351

Garcia, C. (2012, May 16). Chuck D on Obama's gay marriage stance: 'Inevitable and necessary'. Retrieved from https://thegrio.com/2012/05/16/chuck-d-on-obamas-gay-marriage-stance-inevitable-and-necessary/

Garrett-Walker, J. J., & Torres, V. M. (2016). Negative religious rhetoric in the lives of Black cisgender queer emerging adult men: A qualitative analysis. *Journal of Homosexuality*, *64*(13), 1816–1831. doi: 10.1080/00918369. 2016.1267465

George Mason University (n.d.). Retrieved from https://lgbtq.gmu.edu/ programs-services/national-coming-out-day/

Germer, C. K., & Neff, K. D. (2013). Self-compassion in clinical practice. *Journal of Clinical Psychology*, *69*(8), 856–867. doi: 10.1002/jclp.22021

Gilbert, P., & Miles, J. N. V. (2000). Sensitivity to social put-down: It's relationship to perceptions of social rank, shame, social anxiety, depression, anger and self-other blame. *Personality and Individual Differences*, *29*(4), 757–774. https://doi.org/10.1016/s0191-8869(99)00230-5

GLAAD (2019). Where we are on TV 2019–2020. GLAAD. Available at: https://www.glaad.org/whereweareontv19 (accessed 19 April 2020).

Goode-Cross, D. T., & Tager, D. (2011). Negotiating multiple identities: How African-American gay and bisexual men persist at a predominantly white institution. *Journal of Homosexuality*, *58*(9), 1235–1254. doi: 10.1080/0091 8369.2011.605736

Graham, L. (1999). *Our kind of people: Inside America's black upper class* (1st ed.). HarperCollins.

Grant, P. (2016). It's my house and I live here: Using autoethnography to investigate the spaces available for Black male sexual exploration. *Journal of Black Sexuality and Relationships 3*(1), 63–75.

Grant, P. (2018). "Some 'Black gay fantasy'": An exploratory study of discrimination and identity-appraisal among Black same gender loving men. *Journal of Black Sexuality and Relationships*, *4*(3), 49–72.

Grant, P. (2019). Bussinismus: An introduction to the pleasure, pain, power, and politics of bottoming. *Journal of Black Sexuality and Relationships*, *6*(4), 1–26. https://doi.org/10.1353/bsr.2019.0024

Grant, P. (2020a). A new renaissance: Podcasting as a tool to provide nuanced voice to the Black gay male experience. In J. Wadley (Ed.), *Handbook of Sexuality Leadership: Inspiring Community engagement, social empowerment, and transformational influence* (1st ed., pp. 241–262). essay, Routledge.

Grant, P. R. (2020b). Examining internalized homonegativity: Narratives of same sex attracted Black men. *Journal of Black Sexuality and Relationships*, *7*(2), 25–53. https://doi.org/10.1353/bsr.2020.0016

Grant, P., & Francis, S. (2021). Demisexuality. In H. L. Armstrong (Ed.), *Encyclopedia of sex and sexuality: Understanding biology, psychology, and culture* (pp. 157–158). essay, Greenwood.

Griffin, H. L. (2010). *Their own receive them not: African American lesbians and gays in Black churches*. Eugene, OR: Wipf & Stock.

Griffith, J. (2019, April 24). Mother of gay Alabama teen who died by suicide hopes his death encourages tolerance. Retrieved from https://www.nbcnews. com/feature/nbc-out/mother-gay-alabama-teen-who-died-suicide-hopes-his-death-n998056

Griffith, K. H., & Hebl, M. R. (2002). The disclosure dilemma for gay men and lesbians: "Coming out" at work. *Journal of Applied Psychology, 87*(6), 1191–1199.

Hale, S. E., & Ojeda, T. (2018). Acceptable femininity? Gay male misogyny and the policing of queer femininities. *The European Journal of Women's Studies, 25*(3), 310–324. doi: 10.1177/1350506818764762

Han, C. (2015). No brokeback for black men: Pathologizing black male (homo)sexuality through down low discourse. *Social Identities, 21*(3), 228–243. doi: 10.1080/13504630.2015.1041019

Harris, R., & Hayes, S. C. (2019). *ACT made simple: An easy-to-read primer on acceptance and commitment therapy*. New Harbinger Publications.

Haydon, K. C., Collins, W. A., Salvatore, J. E., Simpson, J. A., & Roisman, G. I. (2012). Shared and distinctive origins and correlates of adult attachment representations: The developmental organization of romantic functioning: Adult attachment representations. *Child Development, 83*(5), 1689–1702. doi: 10.1111/j.1467-8624.2012.01801.x

Heard Harvey, Courtney C. C., & Ricard, R. J. (2018). Contextualizing the concept of intersectionality: Layered identities of African American women and gay men in the black church. *Journal of Multicultural Counseling and Development, 46*(3), 206–218. doi: 10.1002/jmcd.12102

Herek, G. M. (2000). The psychology of sexual prejudice. *Current Directions in Psychological Science: A Journal of the American Psychological Society, 9*(1), 19–22. doi: 10.1111/1467-8721.00051

Herek, G. M. (2015). Beyond "homophobia": Thinking more clearly about stigma, prejudice, and sexual orientation. *American Journal of Orthopsychiatry, 85*(5S), S29–S37. doi: 10.1037/ort0000092

Hoefer, S. E., & Hoefer, R. (2017). Worth the wait? The consequences of abstinence-only sex education for marginalized students. *American Journal of Sexuality Education, 12*(3), 257–276. doi: 10.1080/15546128.2017.1359802

Holland, B. (2017, August 29). The 'father of modern gynecology' performed shocking experiments on enslaved women. Retrieved from https://www.history.com/news/the-father-of-modern-gynecology-performed-shocking-experiments-on-slaves

hooks, B. (2004). *We real cool: Black men and masculinity*. New York, NY: Routledge. doi: 10.4324/9780203642207

Horn, A. J., & Wong, Y. J. (2014). Fathering gay sons: A typology of fathering concerns and clinical recommendations. *Professional Psychology, Research and Practice, 45*(4), 247–257. doi: 10.1037/a0037632

Hoskin, R. A. (2019). Femmephobia: The role of anti-femininity and gender policing in LGBTQ+ People's experiences of discrimination. *Sex Roles, 81*(11), 686–703. doi: 10.1007/s11199-019-01021-3

Hudson, T. (2020). Video of Darrel Walls of the Walls Group kissing a man leaked online. Retrieved from https://madamenoire.com/1204248/darrel-walls-kissing-man/

Hughey, M. W., Parks, G. S., & Skocpol, T. (2011). *Black Greek-letter organizations 2.0: New directions in the study of African American fraternities and sororities*. Jackson: University Press of Mississippi.

Hui, M., & Jackson, B. (2017). Looking for brothers: Black male bonding at a predominantly white institution. *The Journal of Negro Education, 86*(4), 463–478. doi: 10.7709/jnegroeducation.86.4.0463

Human Rights Campaign (2015; 2020). Addressing anti-trandgender violence. http://assets2.hrc.org/files/assets/resources/HRC-AntiTransgenderViolence-0519.pdf?_ga=2.187502176.954358560.1623631129-183939496.1623631129; https://www.hrc.org/resources/violence-against-the-trans-and-gender-nonconforming-community-in-2020

Hunter, A. G., & Davis, J. E. (1992). Constructing gender: An exploration of Afro-American men's conceptualization of manhood. *Gender & Society, 6*(3), 464–479. doi: 10.1177/089124392006003007

Hunter, M. A. (2010). All the gays are White and all the Blacks are straight: Black gay men, identity, and community. *Sexuality Research & Social Policy: A Journal of the NSRC, 7*(2), 81–92. doi: 10.1007/s13178-010-0011-4

Hussen, S. A., Gilliard, D., Caldwell, C. H., Andes, K., Chakraborty, R., & Malebranche, D. J. (2014). A qualitative analysis of father–son relationships among HIV-positive young black men who have sex with men. *Journal of Urban Health, 91*(4), 776–792. doi: 10.1007/s11524-013-9864-1

Idsoe, T., Vaillancourt, T., Dyregrov, A., Hagen, K. A., Ogden, T., & Nærde, A. (2021). Bullying victimization and trauma. *Frontiers in Psychiatry, 11.* https://doi.org/10.3389/fpsyt.2020.480353

Irizarry, Y. A., & Perry, R. K. (2017). Challenging the black church narrative: Race, class, and homosexual attitudes. *Journal of Homosexuality, 65*(7), 884–911. https://doi.org/10.1080/00918369.2017.1364566

Jadwin-Cakmak, L. A., Pingel, E. S., Harper, G. W., & Bauermeister, J. A. (2015). Coming out to dad: Young gay and bisexual men's experiences disclosing same-sex attraction to their fathers. *American Journal of Men's Health, 9*(4), 274–288. doi: 10.1177/1557988314539993

Jagger, G. (2008). *Judith Butler: Sexual politics, social change and the power of the performative*. London: Routledge.

James, W. (1902). *The varieties of religious experience: A study in human nature: Being the Gifford Lectures on natural religion delivered at Edinburgh in 1901-1902*. New York; London: Longmans, Green.

Jeffries, W. L., Dodge, B., & Sandfort, T. G. M. (2008). Religion and spirituality among bisexual black men in the USA. *Culture, Health & Sexuality, 10*(5), 463–477. doi: 10.1080/13691050701877526

Jenkins, B. (2016). *Moonlight*. A24.

Jenkins, R. D. (2012). Black fraternal organizations: Understanding the development of hegemonic masculinity and sexuality. *Journal of African American Studies (New Brunswick, N.J.), 16*(2), 226–235. doi: 10.1007/s12111-010-9149-7

Johnson, E. P. (2012). *Sweet Tea: Black gay men of the South*. University of North Carolina Press.

Jones, J. (2015). The myth of Black gay privilege. Retrieved from https://www.huffpost.com/entry/the-myth-of-black-gay-privilege_b_7107304

Jones, J., & Mosher, W. D. (2013). Fathers' involvement with their children: United States, 2006-2010. *National Health Statistics Reports*, (71), 1–21.

Jones, R. L. (2015). *Black haze: Violence, sacrifice, and manhood in black Greek-letter fraternities*. State University of New York Press.

Kafle, N. P. (2013). Hermeneutic phenomenological research method simplified. *Bodhi: An Interdisciplinary Journal*, *5*(1), 181–200. doi: 10.3126/bodhi.v5i1.8053

Kaminski, E. (2008). *Beautiful bottom, beautiful shame: Where "black" meets "queer"*. University of Chicago Press.

Katz, J. (1995). *The invention of heterosexuality*. Dutton.

Kinsey, A., Pomeroy, W., and Martin, C. (1948). *Sexual behavior in the human male*. Philadelphia: W.B. Saunders.

Kinsey, A., Pomeroy, W., Martin, C., and Gebhard, P. (1953). *Sexual behavior in the human female*. Philadelphia: W.B. Saunders.

Krafft-Ebing, R. V., & M., S. K. (1926). *Psychopathia sexualis*. Budapest: Nova.

Lanfranco, F., Kamischke, A., Zitzmann, M., & Nieschlag, E. (2004). Klinefelter's syndrome. *The Lancet (British Edition)*, *364*(9430), 273–283. doi: 10.1016/S0140-6736(04)16678-6

Lasala, M. C., & Frierson, D. T. (2012). African American gay youth and their families: Redefining masculinity, coping with racism and homophobia. *Journal of GLBT Family Studies*, *8*(5), 428–445. doi: 10.1080/1550428X.2012.729948

Lavietes, M. (2019). Tensions between trans women and gay men boil over at Stonewall anniversary. Retrieved from https://www.reuters.com/article/us-gay-pride-transgender/tensions-between-trans-women-and-gay-men-boil-over-at-stonewall-anniversary-idUSKCN1TV0V0

Leary, M. R. (1983). A brief version of the fear of negative evaluation scale. *Personality and Social Psychology Bulletin*, *9*, 371–376.

Lefevor, G. T., Paiz, J. Y., Stone, W., Huynh, K. D., Virk, H. E., Sorrell, S. A., & Gage, S. E. (2020). Homonegativity and the black church: Is congregational variation the missing link? *The Counseling Psychologist*, *48*(6), 826–851. doi: 10.1177/0011000020918558

Lemelle, A. J., & Battle, J. (2004). Black masculinity matters in attitudes toward gay males. *Journal of Homosexuality*, *47*(1), 39–51. https://doi.org/10.1300/j082v47n01_03

Lemelle, A. J. (2010). *Black masculinity and sexual politics*. New York: Routledge. doi: 10.2979/spectrum.1.1.202

Lewis, G. B. (2003). Black-white differences in attitudes toward homosexuality and gay rights. *Public Opinion Quarterly*, *67*(1), 59–78. https://doi.org/10.1086/346009

Linehan, M. (1993). *Cognitive behavioral treatment of borderline personality disorder.* New York: Guilford Press. This is the original textbook (DBT "Bible") where Linehan fleshes out DBT for therapists.

Linehan, M. (2017). *DBT skills training manual.* New York: GUILFORD.

Liptak, A. (2020, June 15). *Civil rights law protects gay and transgender workers, Supreme Court rules.* New York Times. https://www.nytimes.com/2020/06/15/us/gay-transgender-workers-supreme-court.html

Loiacano, D. K. (1989). Gay identity issues among Black Americans: Racism, homophobia, and the need for validation. *Journal of Counseling & Development, 68*(1), 21–25. doi: 10.1002/j.1556-6676.1989.tb02486.x

Mack, N., Woodsong, C., MacQueen, K. M., Guest, G., Namey, E. (2005). *Qualitative research methods: A data collector's field guide.* North Carolina: Family Health International

Maggiora Vergano, C., Lauriola, M., & Speranza, A. M. (2015). The complex trauma questionnaire (ComplexTQ): Development and preliminary psychometric properties of an instrument for measuring early relational trauma. *Frontiers in Psychology, 6,* 1323- 1323. doi: 10.3389/fpsyg.2015.01323

Manago, C. (1996). Manhood-who claims it? who does it claim? *The Black Scholar, 26*(1), 48–49. doi: 10.1080/00064246.1996.11430774

Mantzoukas, S., Kotrotsiou, S., Mentis, M., Paschou, A., Diamantopoulos, E., Kotrotsiou, E., & Gouva, M. (2021). Exploring the impact of shame on health-related quality of life in older individuals. *Journal of Nursing Scholarship,* 10.1111/jnu.12663

Marshall, B. D., Shannon, K., Kerr, T., Zhang, R., Wood, E. (2010). Survival sex work and increased HIV risk among sexual minority street-involved youth. *Journal of Acquired Immune Deficiency Syndrome,* 2010; *53*(5):661–664. doi: 10.1097/QAI.0b013e3181c300d7

Martinez, O. (2020). The effects of three types of sexual orientation victimization on HIV sexual risk behavior among Black South African men who have sex with men (MSM). *Journal of Homosexuality, 67*(4), 513–527. doi: 10.1080/00918369.2018.1547561. Epub 2018 Dec 24. PMID: 30582734.

Mayfield, W. (2001). The development of an internalized homonegativity inventory for gay men. *Journal of Homosexuality, 41,* 53–76.

Mays, V. M., Cochran, S. D., & Barnes, N. W. (2007). Race, race-based discrimination, and health outcomes among African Americans. *Annual Review of Psychology, 58,* 201–225. doi: 10.1146/annurev.psych.57.102904.190212

McClure, S. M. (2006). Improvising masculinity: African American fraternity membership in the construction of a Black masculinity. *Journal of African American Studies, 10,* 57–73.

McGuire, K. M., Berhanu, J., Davis, C. H. F., & Harper, S. R. (2014). In search of progressive black masculinities: Critical self-reflections on gender identity development among black undergraduate men. *Men and Masculinities, 17*(3), 253–277. doi: 10.1177/1097184X13514055

McKaiser, E. (2012, October 02). Homosexuality un-African? The claim is an historical embarrassment. Retrieved from https://www.theguardian.com/world/2012/oct/02/homosexuality-unafrican-claim-historical-embarrassment

McKay, T., & Angotti, N. (2016). Ready rhetorics: Political homophobia and activist discourses in Malawi, Nigeria, and Uganda. *Qualitative Sociology*, *39*(4), 397–420. doi: 10.1007/s11133-016-9342-7

McLaren, A. (1997). *The trials of masculinity: Policing sexual boundaries, 1870-1930*. University of Chicago Press.

McCune, J. Q. (2008). "Out" in the club: The down low, hip-hop, and the architexture of Black Masculinity. *Text and Performance Quarterly*, *28*(3), 298–314. doi: 10.1080/10462930802107415

McCune, J. Q. (2014). *Sexual discretion. Black masculinity and the politics of passing*. Chicago: University of Chicago Press.

Mendoza-Denton, R., Downey, G., Purdie, V. J., Davis, A., & Pietrzak, J. (2002). Sensitivity to status-based rejection: Implications for African American students' college experience. *Journal of Personality and Social Psychology*, *83*(4), 896–918. doi: 10.1037/0022-3514.83.4.896

Mereish, E. H., Sheskier, M., Hawthorne, D. J., & Goldbach, J. T. (2019). Sexual orientation disparities in mental health and substance use among black American young people in the USA: Effects of cyber and bias-based victimisation. *Culture, Health & Sexuality*, *21*(9), 985–998. doi: 10.1080/13691058.2018.1532113

Mersky, J. P., Topitzes, J., & Reynolds, A. J. (2013). Impacts of adverse childhood experiences on health, mental health, and substance use in early adulthood: A cohort study of an urban, minority sample in the U.S. *Child Abuse & Neglect*, *37*(11), 917–925. doi: 10.1016/j.chiabu.2013.07.011

Meyer, I. H. (1995). Minority stress and mental health in gay men. *Journal of Health and Social Behavior*, *36*(1), 38–56. doi: 10.2307/2137286

Meyer, I. H. (2003). Prejudice, social stress, and mental health in lesbian, gay, and bisexual populations: Conceptual issues and research evidence. *Psychological Bulletin*, *129*(5), 674–697. doi: 10.1037/0033-2909.129.5.674

Meyer, I. H. (2015). Resilience in the study of minority stress and health of sexual and gender minorities. *Psychology of Sexual Orientation and Gender Diversity*, *2*(3), 209–213. doi: 10.1037/sgd0000132

Miller, R. L., Jr (2007). Legacy denied: African American gay men, AIDS, and the black church. *Social work*, *52*(1), 51–61. https://doi.org/10.1093/sw/52.1.51

Millett, G., Malebranche, D., Mason, B., & Spikes, P. (2006). Focusing down low: Bisexual black men, HIV risk and heterosexual transmission. *Journal of the National Medical Association*, *97*(7) Press. https://www.jstor.org/stable/10.5149/9781469626857_mumford

Money, J., Hampson, J. G., & Hampson, J. L. (1955). Hermaphroditism: Recommendations concerning assignment of sex, change of sex and psychologic management. *Bulletin of the Johns Hopkins Hospital*, *97*(4), 284–300.

Money, J., Hampson, J. G., & Hampson J. L. (1957). Imprinting and the establishment of gender role. *A.M.A. Archives of Neurology and Psychiatry*, *77*(3), 333–336. doi: 10.1001/archneurpsyc.1957.02330330119019

Monteiro, K. P., & Fuqua, V. (1993). African American gay youth: One form of manhood. *The High School Journal, 77*(1/2), 20–36.

Moore, S., Jones, M., Smith, J. C., Hood, J., Harper, G. W., Camacho-Gonzalez, A., del Rio, C., & Hussen, S. A. (2019). Homonegativity experienced over the life course by young black gay, bisexual and other men who have sex with men (YB-GBMSM) living with HIV in Atlanta, Georgia. *AIDS and Behavior, 23*(S3), 266–275. doi: 10.1007/s10461-019-02658-7

Moore, S. E., Robinson, M. A., Dailey, A., & Thompson, C. (2015). Suffering in silence: Child sexual molestation and the black church: If God don't help me who can I turn to? *Journal of Human Behavior in the Social Environment, 25*(2), 147–157. doi: 10.1080/10911359.2014.956962

Morales E. S. (1989) Ethnic minority families and minority gays and lesbians. *Marriage & Family Review, 14*(3–4) 217–239. doi: 10.1300/J002v14n03_11

Morrow, S. L. (2000). First do no harm: Therapists issues in psychotherapy with lesbian, gay and bisexual clients. In R. M. Perez, K. A. DeBord, & K. J. Bieschke (Eds.), *Handbook of counseling and psychotherapy with lesbian, gay, and bisexual clients* (pp. 137–156). Washington, DC: American Psychological Association.

Moseby, K. M. (2017). Two regimes of HIV/AIDS: The MMWR and the socio-political construction of HIV/AIDS as a 'black disease'. *Sociology of Health & Illness, 39*(7), 1068–1082. doi: 10.1111/1467-9566.12552

Mumford, K. (2016). *Not straight, not white: Black gay men from the march on Washington to the AIDS crisis.* (John Hope Franklin Series in African American History and Culture). University of North Carolina

Munzenrieder, K. (2012). FAMU hazing homicide victim Robert Champion might have been targeted because he was gay. Retrieved from https://www.miaminewtimes.com/news/famu-hazing-homicide-victim-robert-champion-might-have-been-targeted-because-he-was-gay-6551326

Muparamoto, N. (2020). LGBT individuals and the struggle against Robert Mugabe's extirpation in Zimbabwe. *Africa Review (New Delhi), 116.* 10.1080/09744053.2020.1812042

Murray, S. O., Roscoe, W., & Epprecht, M. (2021). *Boy-wives and female husbands: Studies in African homosexualities.* Albany: State University of New York Press.

Neff, K. D. (2003). Self-compassion: An alternative conceptualization of a healthy attitude toward oneself. *Self and Identity, 2*, 85–102.

Nelson, K. M., Pantalone, D. W., & Carey, M. P. (2019). Sexual health education for adolescent males who are interested in sex with males: An investigation of experiences, preferences, and needs. *Journal of Adolescent Health, 64*(1), 36–42. 10.1016/j.jadohealth.2018.07.015

Nero, C. I. (2005). Why are gay ghettoes white? *A Critical Anthology Black Queer Studies, 228*–248. doi: 10.1215/9780822387220-013

Nederveen Pieterse, J. (1992). *White on black: Images of Africa and Blacks in western popular culture.* New Haven: Yale University Press.

Nieschlag, E. (2013). Klinefelter syndrome: The commonest form of hypogonadism, but often overlooked or untreated. *Deutsches Ärzteblatt International, 110*(20), 347–353. doi: 10.3238/arztebl.2013.0347

O'Donnell, S., Meyer, I. H., & Schwartz, S. (2011). Increased risk of suicide attempts among black and Latino lesbians, gay men, and bisexuals. *American Journal of Public Health (1971), 101*(6), 1055–1059. doi: 10.2105/AJPH.2010.300032

Obergefell v. Hodges, 576 U.S.___ (2015) https://supreme.justia.com/cases/federal/us/576/14-556/

OUT Right Action International (2020, February 18). Acronyms Explained. Retrieved from https://outrightinternational.org/content/acronyms-explained

Pachankis, J. E., Hatzenbuehler, M. L., Rendina, H. J., Safren, S. A., & Parsons, J. T. (2015). LGB-affirmative cognitive-behavioral therapy for young adult gay and bisexual men: A randomized controlled trial of a transdiagnostic minority stress approach. *Journal of Consulting and Clinical Psychology, 83*(5), 875–889. doi: 10.1037/ccp0000037

Parkinson, J. (2016, January 07). The significance of Sarah Baartman. Retrieved from https://www.bbc.com/news/magazine-35240987

Pascoe, C. J. (2011). *Dude, you're a fag.* University of California Press.

Pedulla, D. S. (2014). The positive consequences of negative stereotypes: Race, sexual orientation, and the job application process. *Social Psychology Quarterly, 77*(1), 75–94. doi: 10.1177/0190272513506229

Pelzer, D. (2016). Creating a new narrative: Reframing black masculinity for college men. *The Journal of Negro Education, 85*(1), 16–27. doi: 10.7709/jnegroeducation.85.1.0016

Phornphutkul, C., Boney, C. M., Fausto-Sterling, A., & Gruppuso, P. A. (1998). Gender assignment at birth: Three cases of Reassignment/Ambiguity at or beyond adolescence. 466. *Pediatric Research, 43*, 82–82. doi: 10.1203/00006450-199804001-00487

Pitt, R. N. (2009). "Still looking for my Jonathan": Gay black men's management of religious and sexual identity conflicts. *Journal of Homosexuality, 57*(1), 39. doi: 10.1080/00918360903285566

Pitt, R. N. (2010). "Killing the messenger": Religious black gay men's neutralization of anti-gay religious messages. *Journal for the Scientific Study of Religion. 49*(1): 56–72. doi: 10.1111/j.1468-5906.2009.01492.x

Poulson-Bryant, S. (2006). *Hung: A meditation on the measure of Black men in America.* New York: Harlem Moon.

Quinn, K., & Dickson-Gomez, J. (2015). Homonegativity, religiosity, and the intersecting identities of young black men who have sex with men. *AIDS and Behavior, 20*(1), 51–64. https://doi.org/10.1007/s10461-015-1200-1

Quinn, K., Dickson-Gomez, J., Difranceisco, W., Kelly, J. A., St. Lawrence, J. S., Amirkhanian, Y. A., & Broaddus, M. (2015). Correlates of internalized homonegativity among Black men who have sex with men. *AIDS Education and Prevention, 27*(3), 212–226. https://doi.org/10.1521/aeap.2015.27.3.212

Ransom, D. (2019, October 22). Tank on same-sex oral intercourse: 'Doesn't mean he's gay'. Retrieved from https://www.bet.com/music/2019/10/22/tank-same-sex-oral-intercourse.html

Reynolds, C. (2015). I am super straight and I prefer you be too: Constructions of heterosexual masculinity in online personal ads for "Straight" men seeking sex with men. *The Journal of Communication Inquiry*, *39*(3), 213–231. doi: 10.1177/0196859915575736

Richardson, M. (2011). Our stories have never been told: Preliminary thoughts on black lesbian cultural production as historiography in "The Watermelon Woman." *Black Camera: An International Film Journal (the New Series)*, *2*(2), 100–113. doi: 10.2979/blackcamera.2.2.100

Robertson, D. L., & Avent, J. R. (2016). African American counselors-in-training, the black church, and lesbian-, gay-, and bisexual-affirmative counseling: Considerations for counselor education programs. *Counseling and Values*, *61*(2), 223–238. doi: 10.1002/cvj.12039

Robinson, R. K. (2009). Racing the closet. *Stanford Law Review*, *61*(6), 1463–1533.

Rosario, M., Rotheram-Borus, M. J., & Reid, H. (1996). Gay-related stress and its correlates among gay and bisexual male adolescents of predominantly Black and Hispanic background. *Journal of Community Psychology*, *24*(2), 136–159. doi: 10.1002/(SICI)15206629(199604)24:2<136::AID-JCOP5>3.0.CO;2-X

Rosenthal, M. S. (2013). *Human sexuality: From cells to society*. Cengage Learning (Firm) Ross

Ross, L. C. (2008). *The divine nine: The history of African American fraternities and sororities*. New York, NY: Kensington Publishing.

Ross, M. B. (2013). "What's love but a second hand emotion?": Man-on-man passion in the contemporary black gay romance novel. *Callaloo*, *36*(3), 669–686. doi: 10.1353/cal.2013.0159

Rumens, N. (2010). Workplace friendships between men: Gay men's perspectives and experiences. *Human Relations*, *63*(10), 1541. doi: 10.1177/0018726710361987

Rumens, N., & Kerfoot, D. (2009). Gay men at work: (Re)constructing the self as professional. *Human Relations*, *62*(5), 763–786. doi: 10.1177/0018726709103457

Rustin, B., Carbado, D. W., & Weise, D. (2015). *Time on two crosses: The collected writings of Bayard Rustin*. Berkeley: Cleis Press.

Safren, S. A., & Rogers, T. (2001). Cognitive-behavioral therapy with gay, lesbian, and bisexual clients. *Journal of Clinical Psychology*, *57*(5), 629–643. doi: 10.1002/jclp.1033

Savin-Williams, R. C. (1994). Verbal and physical abuse as stressors in the lives of lesbian, gay male, and bisexual youths: Associations with school problems, running away, substance abuse, prostitution, and suicide. *Journal of Consulting and Clinical Psychology*, *62*(2), 261–269. doi: 10.1037//0022-006X.62.2.261

Schulte, L. J., & Battle, J. (2004). The relative importance of ethnicity and religion in predicting attitudes towards gays and lesbians. *Journal of Homosexuality*, *47*(2), 127–142. doi: 10.1300/J082v47n02_08

Schwarz, A. B. C. (2003). *Gay voices of the Harlem renaissance*. Bloomington: Indiana University Press.

Scott, A. O. (2016). 'Moonlight': Is this the year's best movie? *New York Times (Online)*.

Shain, B. N. (2019). Increases in rates of suicide and suicide attempts among black adolescents. *Pediatrics (Evanston)*, *144*(5), e20191912. doi: 10.1542/peds.2019-1912

Shoptaw, S., Weiss, R. E., Munjas, B., Hucks-Ortiz, C., Young, S. D., Larkins, S., ... Gorbach, P. M. (2009). Homonegativity, substance use, sexual risk behaviors, and HIV status in poor and ethnic men who have sex with men in Los Angeles. *Journal of Urban Health*, *86*(S1), 77–92. doi: 10.1 007/s11524-009-9372-5

Skock, I. R. (2021, May 30). Robert Mugabe: 25-years of gay-bashing. Retrieved April 28, 2021, from https://www.pri.org/stories/2012-05-30/robert-mugabe-25-years-gay-bashing

Slatton, B. C., & Spates, K. (2014; 2016). *Hyper sexual, hyper masculine?: Gender, race and sexuality in the identities of contemporary black men*. Routledge. doi: 10.4324/9781315587691

Smyth, C. (1990). The pleasure threshold: Looking at lesbian pornography on film. *Feminist Review*, (34), 152–159. doi: 10.2307/1395314

Snorton, C. (2014). *Nobody is supposed to know: Black sexuality on the down low*. Minneapolis; London: University of Minnesota Press. Retrieved June 13, 2021, from http://www.jstor.org/stable/10.5749/j.ctt6wr7jt

Soldati-Kahimbaara, K. (2016). Parental 'coming out': The journeys of Black South African mothers through their personal narratives. *South African Review of Sociology*, *47*(3), 110–128. doi: 10.1080/21528586.2016.1182443

Somé, M. P. (1993). "Gays as spiritual gatekeepers." *White Crane Newsletter* *4*(9): 1,6,8. (Interview of Somé by Bert Hoff).

Stack, L. (2020, July 01). Overlooked no more: Karl Heinrich Ulrichs, pioneering gay activist. Retrieved from https://www.nytimes.com/2020/07/01/obituaries/karl-heinrich-ulrichs-overlooked.html

Smith, S. L., Choueiti, M., & Pieper, K. (2016) *Inclusion or invisibility? Comprehensive Annenberg report on diversity in entertainment*. Los Angeles, CA: USC Annenberg.

Stefanou, C., & McCabe, M. P. (2012). Adult attachment and sexual functioning: A review of past research. *The Journal of Sexual Medicine*, *9*(10), 2499–2507. doi: 10.1111/j.17436109.2012.02843.x

Stoler, A. L. (1989). Making empire respectable: The politics of race and sexual morality in 20th-century colonial cultures. *American Ethnologist*, *16*(4), 634–660. https://doi.org/10.1525/ae.1989.16.4.02a00030

Stone, B. E. (2011). The down low and the sexuality of Race. *Foucault Studies*, 36–50. https://doi.org/10.22439/fs.v0i12.3332

Stoller, R. J. (1990). *Sex and gender*. Karnac.

Stone, A. L., & Ward, J. (2011). From 'black people are not a homosexual act' to 'gay is the new black': Mapping white uses of blackness in modern gay rights campaigns in the United States. *Social Identities, 17*(5), 605–624. doi: 10.1080/13504630.2011.595204

Strayhorn, T. L., Blakewood, A. M., & DeVita, J. M. (2008). Factors affecting the college choice of African American gay male undergraduates: Implications for retention. *National Association of Student Affairs Professionals, 11*(1), 88–108.

Strayhorn, T. L., & Tillman-Kelly, D. L. (2013). Queering masculinity: Manhood and black gay men in college. *Spectrum: A Journal on Black Men, 1*(2), 83–110.

Summers, M. A. (2004). *Manliness and its discontents: The Black middle class and the transformation of masculinity, 1900-1930*. Chapel Hill: University of North Carolina Press.

Szymanski, D. M., Kashubeck-West, S., & Meyer, J. (2008). Internalized heterosexism: A historical and theoretical overview. *The Counseling Psychologist, 36*(4), 510–524. doi: 10.1177/0011000007309488

Tamale, S. (2014, April 26). Homosexuality is not un-African. Retrieved April 28, 2021, from http://america.aljazeera.com/opinions/2014/4/homosexuality-africamuseveniugandanigeriaethiopia.html

The Black Effect (Producer) (2017-2021). Whoreible Decisions Podcast. https://podcasts.apple.com/us/podcast/whoreible-decisions/id1224239045

Tennial, D. (2015). *Marginalized men: Stories of SGL ministers in the African American church*. Atlanta: DT Media.

Tennial, D. M. (2014). Don't ask, don't tell: The unspoken policy of the African American church in the south. *Counterpoints (New York, N.Y.), 434*, 190–197.

The Genderbread Person. Retrieved from https://www.genderbread.org/

The Source (2021). Donnie McClurkin Says He's 'Delivered' From Homosexuality. Retrieved from https://thesource.com/2021/03/31/donnie-mcclurkin-says-hes-delivered-from-homosexuality/

The Trevor Project (2020). All Black lives matter: Mental health of Black LGBTQ youth. Retrieved from https://www.thetrevorproject.org/2020/10/06/all-black-lives-matter-mental-health-of-black-lgbtq-youth/

Thurman, W., Hughes, L., Hurston, Z. N., Bennett, G., Bruce, R., Cullen, C., & Douglas, A. (1926). *Fire!!: A quarterly devoted to the younger Negro artists*. Elizabeth, NJ: FIRE!! Press.

Tobia, J. (2016, May 12). Gender neutral pronouns: How to use the right pronouns. Retrieved from https://time.com/4327915/gender-neutral-pronouns/

Totenhagen, C. J., Randall, A. K., & Lloyd, K. (2018). Stress and relationship functioning in same-sex couples: The vulnerabilities of internalized homophobia and outness: Stress and relationship functioning in same-sex couples. *Family Relations, 67*(3), 399–413. doi: 10.1111/fare.12311

Totten, P. (2015). A man should never eat a pickle in public: A black man's understanding of enactments of gender and sexuality. *Creative Approaches to Research, 8*(2), 4.

Travers, C. (2019). Theorizing manhood, masculinities and mindset among black male undergraduate students. *The Journal of Negro Education, 88*(1), 32–43. doi: 10.7709/jnegroeducation.88.1.0032

Troiden, R. R. (1989a). *Gay and lesbian identity: A sociological analysis.* New York: General Hall.

Troiden, R. R. (1989b). The formation of homosexual identities. *Journal of Homosexuality, 17*(1/2), 43–73. doi: 10.1300/J082v17n01_02

Trujillo, M. A., Perrin, P. B., Henry, R. S., & Rabinovitch, A. E. (2020). Heterosexism and suicidal ideation: Racial differences in the impact of social support among sexual minority adults. *Crisis: The Journal of Crisis Intervention and Suicide Prevention, 41*(6), 429–436. doi: 10.1027/0227-5910/a000657

United States Department of Justice (2020). Grand jury charges Ed Buck with four additional felonies, including that he enticed victims to travel interstate to engage in prostitution. Retrieved from https://www.justice.gov/usao-cdca/pr/grand-jury-charges-ed-buck-four-additional-felonies-including-he-enticed-victims-travel

University of California Davis (2019, November 26). Pronouns. Retrieved from https://lgbtqia.ucdavis.edu/educated/pronouns

Van der Feltz-Cornelis, Christina M, Potters, E. C., van Dam, A., Koorndijk, R. P. M., Elfeddali, I., & van Eck van der Sluijs, Jonna F. (2018, 2019). Adverse childhood experiences (ACE) in outpatients with anxiety and depressive disorders and their association with psychiatric and somatic comorbidity and revictimization. Cross-sectional observational study. *Journal of Affective Disorders, 246*, 458–464. doi: 10.1016/j.jad.2018.12.096

VanManen, M. (1990). *Researching lived experience: Human science for an action sensitive pedagogy.* Albany: State Univ. of New York Pr.

Walker, J. N. J., & Longmire-Avital, B. (2013). The impact of religious faith and internalized homonegativity on resiliency for black lesbian, gay, and bisexual emerging adults. *Developmental Psychology, 49*(9), 1723–1731. https://doi.org/10.1037/a0031059

Wang, C., Lin, H., Chen, M., Ko, N., Chang, Y., Lin, I., & Yen, C. (2018). Effects of traditional and cyber homophobic bullying in childhood on depression, anxiety, and physical pain in emerging adulthood and the moderating effects of social support among gay and bisexual men in Taiwan. *Neuropsychiatric Disease and Treatment, 14*, 1309–1317. doi: 10.2147/NDT.S164579

Ward, E. G. (2005). Homophobia, hypermasculinity and the US black church. *Culture, Health & Sexuality, 7*(5), 493–504. doi: 10.1080/13691050500151248

Ward, J. (2008). White normativity: The cultural dimensions of whiteness in a racially diverse LGBT organization. *Sociological Perspectives, 51*(3), 563–586. doi: 10.1525/sop.2008.51.3.563

Weeks, J. H. (1909). "Anthropological notes on the Bangala of the Upper Congo River." *Journal of the Anthropological Institute of Great Britain and Ireland, 39*: 97-136, 416–459.

Wheeler, D. P., Millett, G. A., Carson, L. F., Liau, A., Bond, L., & LaPollo, A. B. (2009). Black men who have sex with men and the association of down-low identity with HIV risk behavior (Research and Practice) (author abstract). *American Journal of Public Health (1971)*, *99*(4), S92.

White, J. J., Dangerfield, D. T., Donovan, E., Miller, D., & Grieb, S. M. (2019). Exploring the role of LGBT-affirming churches in health promotion for black sexual minority men. *Culture, Health & Sexuality*, 1–16. doi: 10.1 080/13691058.2019.1666429

Whiting, G. W., & Lewis, T. (2008). On manliness: Black masculinity revisited. *AMQST AmeriQuests*, *6*(1). doi: 10.15695/amqst.v6i1.153

Wilkerson, J. M., Smolenski, D. J., Brady, S. S., & Rosser, B. R. S. (2012). Religiosity, internalized homonegativity and outness in Christian men who have sex with men. *Sexual and Relationship Therapy*, *27*(2), 122–132. doi: 10.1080/14681994.2012.698259

Winder, T. J. A. (2015). "Shouting it out": Religion and the development of Black gay identities. *Qualitative Sociology*, *38*(4), 375. doi: 10.1007/s11133-015-9316-1

Witherspoon, C. (2015). Kirk Franklin apologizes to gay community for 'homophobia' in Black church. Retrieved from https://thegrio.com/2015/11/12/kirk-franklin-apology-homophobia-black-church-gay-community/

Wolitski, R. J., Jones, K. T., Wasserman, J. L., & Smith, J. C. (2006). Self-identification as "Down low" among men who have sex with men (MSM) from 12 US cities. *AIDS and Behavior*, *10*(5), 519–529. doi: 10.1007/s10461-006-9095-5

Index

Note: Italicized page numbers refer to table. Page numbers followed by "n" refer to notes.

For Product Safety Concerns and Information please contact our EU
representative GPSR@taylorandfrancis.com
Taylor & Francis Verlag GmbH, Kaufingerstraße 24, 80331 München, Germany

www.ingramcontent.com/pod-product-compliance
Lightning Source LLC
Chambersburg PA
CBHW061744270326
41928CB00011B/2374